A Sentence with the District

by Alberto "Beto" Gutierrez

First published by Alberto "Beto" Gutierrez and printed by
Lulu Press in 2007.

ISBN: 978-0-6152-3585-1

Library of Congress Control Number: 2008906383

Cover Design by Beto Gutierrez

My work is dedicated to all of my students who also have been my favorite teachers. This particular project has a very special dedication to Lisbeth Flores, a young woman who taught me the value of each day. She fought to stay alive, as I have seen no one else do. Lisbeth passed of leukemia at the young age of 15.

Acknowledgements

I am blessed to be surrounded with an amazing group of people who have supported and contributed to this book in more ways than one. The following is a partial list of people who played key roles throughout this amazing journey.

To my friend Lorena Torres, you have been my biggest cheerleader and sounding board since the start of the project. Natalia Pedrani, you have encouraged me persistently to complete this project and I thank you for having assisted in translating the book.

To my parents, Cesario Gutierrez and Braulia Lozano for having the patience to see me grow into the man I have become.

To my siblings, Armando, Gustavo, Antonia, and Alejandro, thank you for enduring the big brother that I am.

To my beautiful nephews and niece, Tupac Amaru, Mando (a.k.a. Choncho), and Maya for your unconditional love, innocence, and the joy you bring to the family – you are all a fun bunch.

To my tía Sylvia for your commitment to our grandparents and your unconditional love to the entire family.

To my Godparents Jose and Petra Menchaca who played a pivotal role throughout my college years. Thank you for opening your home.

To Cesar Menchaca, the father/friend/son/cousin/charro who has played the role of my older brother.

To my tíos Pancho, Piri, and Pifas for stepping up and supporting me when I was in college.

To my tía Pancha for being the first in the family to reach out to me during the hardest times.

To my first mentors in college, Cuco Lepe, Ernesto Ortega, and Ramiro Barragan, THANK YOU!

To Diedra Shumate, many thanks for your written contribution to this book and ongoing support.

To my colleagues who supported me until my very last day at SFHS. Thank you Diane Hernandez, Sylvia Suarez, Lydia Soto, Jose Garcia, Susana Hernandez, Robert Mitchell, Alvaro Holguin, Coach Chapman, and Ms. Naz.

The following is a partial list of friends and family who did not allow me to give up when exhaustion wanted to take over. You served as a fountain of inspiration to complete the book. Ana Aguilar, Angela Acosta, Alberto and Rosie Botero, Alex and Daniel Cendejas, Audra and Lorraine Tabarez, Belinda Barragán, Beto Menchaca, Carmen Beltran, Elizabeth Morín, Esq. Humberto Guizar, Ivan Sanchez, Dr. Jackie Leavitt, Janet Ceja, Javier Flores, Jim Walker, Joaquin Chavez, Dr. Jorge Haddock, Dr. Leo Estrada, Luis Rodríguez, Marco Torres, Maria Barajas, Magali Zapien, Margo Magdi, Maribel Garcia, Maria Mendoza, Maria Luisa Valenzuela, Melissa Castrellon, Myrna Martinez, my angel Norma Vega, Rosa Gonzalez, Verónica Rivas, Ms. Cunningham, Todd Tyni, Greg Solkovitz, Donna Finklestein, LP45 and LP65.

To all of the students who day in and day out provided me with the stories that informed this project. I'm also grateful to the students who openly supported my vision for a better educational system – Maribel, Janet, Oscar, Vicky, Melissa, Rosa, Diana, Vince, Ricardo, Rigo, Carlos, Suhey, Luis, Carlota, Ana, Jason, Jazzmin, Angelica, Cynthia, Karla, China, Manuel, Jr., Natalia, Myrna, Fabiola, Veterano, Christian, Jose, Maria, Jesus, Adan, Daniel, Alex, Jeannette, Glendy, Tony, Jessica, Jackie, Sergio, Erika, Mayra, Mike, Juanita, Linda, Adam, Billy, Nancy, Angel, Carmelo, Marisol, Laura, Oscar, Brenda, Adriana, Claudia, Areli, Miriam, Lily, Mauro, Marisol, Sandra, Yesenia, Miguel, Abigail, Gilberto, Mario, Mauricio, Cindy, Trino, Glenda, Elia, Marisol, Colocho, Ruby, Gabriel, Linda, Armando, Richard, Horacio, Olga, Karina, Lorena, Andrew, Abel, Ramon, Raul, Nancy, Julie, Chuy, Alma, Arlene, Joanna, Ashley, Cindy, Pedro, Candido, Candy, Nelly, Dorian, Leticia, Hugo, Mario, Diego, Eric, Sole, Martha, Guillermo, Pablo, Reyna, Ruben, Rafael, Sonia, Sarah, Susana, Soledad, Vanessa, Xiomara, Isidro, Elia, and Marvin.

Table of Contents

x

Foreword

Even while they teach, men learn.
-Seneca

      I met Alberto Gutierrez, better known to his family and friends as "Beto," about four years ago after he completed graduate school and was returning to the teaching profession. He struck me then as a man who is passionate in his beliefs and understands the necessity of human connections. Like all new teachers, Beto was full of promise and possibilities in entering such a noble profession. He was going to change the world by having a positive affect on each of the young men and women that would cross over his threshold. The education system, which functions similar to a small government, can become poorly managed, corrupt, and, neglected, leading to indifference among other unfortunate and negative impact. Cronyism plays a part as well. In the world of school superintendents and administrators, this practice is so pervasive and self-generating it excludes teachers and students. The result of this practice is that society pays the price. Poor education has a domino effect directly linked to social and economic non-performance.

      Teaching is an extremely difficult and demanding profession. It is imperative that a new teacher is nurtured, provided with support, given constructive criticism, and effective communication that will allow the teacher to blossom and develop into an individual who can inspire and stimulate the minds that are placed into his/her domain...the classroom. Magic can truly take place within the four walls, provided that the climate and culture of the school is conducive to it. It truly is a trickle down effect. The administrators must be connected to their teachers as support providers and not just disciplinarians who only look to reprimand. They become reactors and tend to forget the process of teaching, which ironically, they were part of at one point in their career. So the question becomes, "What happens in a school system where a once wide-eyed, enthusiastic, and idealistic teacher's spirit becomes broken?" This brings us to Beto's story. His teaching experience was one of restriction. A high school whose system functions much like a prison. One that mentally and emotionally confines, deprives personal freedoms, lacks adequate supervision, and sets a policy of zero expectations. Teachers are to simply sign-in daily and try to maintain decorum. Students need to attend daily so that the school can collect its funds from the state. The concept of "learning" is non-existent. There is no vision for teachers to provide their students with knowledge and goals that can profoundly change their future. With time, the school crumbles under the weight of mediocrity and indifference. All parties simply "show up."

Teaching is a noble profession. One in which you either become an active participant or a spectator in your own classroom. My twenty-five years as an educator in the Los Angeles Unified School District (LAUSD) taught me that in order to inspire students, the teacher must become both – teacher and student. As I reflect back to my beginning, I was a very young and naive teacher, full of idealism and purpose. Unlike Beto, I had a very different experience. I was nurtured, supported and was part of a team community with an altruistic viewpoint that believed that all children had the ability to achieve. This unity provided the opportunity for everyone working in the school community to thrive. High expectations were a given and judgment was not placed on where a student was from, but on the value of their destination. Each teaching year was rewarding and fulfilling. I grew to understand the complexity of teaching and that it is a gift in which one is to handle with care. The ultimate payoff is the love, respect, and loyalty that was freely given to me by the majority of the parents and students. I collaborated, mentored, felt sorrow, and joy. It was not always an easy experience, but one in which truly defined my life's purpose – to touch the lives of others. All teaching experiences are unique to the individual teacher.

A Sentence with the District is a poignant portrait of Beto's life as a teacher at Los Angeles' San Fernando High School. It is his raw, honest, and courageous truth that involves reconciliation of past demons, feelings of disillusionment, and abandonment. This book provides considerable insight into a dysfunctional LAUSD school. Using his own childhood experiences, Beto explores the relationships between family, gangs, poverty and self-doubt. The reader might perceive that Alberto Gutierrez paid a price for teaching at San Fernando High School. However, if the price bought a spiritual awakening of self-love and self-acceptance, then I am sure you would agree that it was well worth it. *A Sentence with the District* is a compelling account of one man's journey of self-discovery.

~ *Diedra Shumate*
Educator

Introduction

This body of work originated in a form different from how it appears today. Originally, the short stories were written for my personal benefit as entries in my journal. My journal served as my confidant and the portal through which my passion, imagination, and frustration alike ran rampant in the safety of blank pages. However, the stories soon came to have an energy, a consciousness of their own and called on me to share my experiences as a student and teacher at LAUSD. While the stories are based on truth and reflect my reality, all the names have been changed to protect the innocent and the not so innocent...

This book is presented in a positive spirit in hopes of shedding light on the everyday life of learning and teaching within the nation's second largest school district, LAUSD. My stories seek to capture and share that which cannot be learned from a textbook or taught in a classroom. They seek to inspire change and advocate a greater awareness of our youth, the education system, and what we can do to contribute to the greater good.

The human experience cannot be justly conveyed by university-generated statistics, especially when most education researchers and or professors have never taught in a K-12 classroom for more than a handful of years. The public school system is a unique institution with many sideline critics who are not willing to get dirty.

Before I joined the district, I was excited to read job postings that invited enthusiastic young adults to teach. My decision to apply was based on the idea that I could make a difference. I wanted to provide a learning environment for teenagers that was different from my own.

My first year was full of surprises. In fact, during my first two years of teaching I was assigned eleven different preparatory courses. I walked around with the spirit of Mexican comedic superhero *El Chapulin Colorado*. I could handle anything. No task was too big and I never said no to any requests. I was assigned Spanish II for Native Speakers my first year. I started during the spring semester and was that class's fifth teacher that year. I am a fluent Spanish speaker, but I knew nothing about Spanish grammar. My specialty was social studies. Actually, I felt uncomfortable speaking Spanish to native speakers. Without much guidance, I had no choice but to turn the class into a speech and debate course where students would use the Spanish language very differently. I encouraged critical thinking in Spanish, something different for all of us. To my surprise, many of my students had signed up to take the Advance Placement (AP) Spanish test. Approximately eighty percent of the students who took the AP test passed. Certainly, I and the other four substitutes had little to do with students passing the exam. I was not even aware that students were planning to take the test, let alone prepare them for it. At the end of the semester, the students were happy that I ended the high turnover of teachers and provided them the consistency they desired for the rest of the semester. I encouraged students to speak up about the high turnover of substitutes. The students refused and were simply content that the semester was over.

At the end of my first semester when final exams were taken, I saw the students walk aimlessly around campus. I was in a state of shock and attempted to remember if that was my experience as a student. I could not remember since I hardly attended school myself. Finals week was a blur. I was shocked to see how indifferent administrators and faculty were about the hundreds of students walking the hallways aimlessly throughout the day. Teachers were busy submitting final grades, while administrators were busy doing administrative work like answering phones, signing papers, having meetings, waiting by the coffee machine, or faxing important papers. The school only gave importance to homeroom. Technically students could miss all other periods but homeroom. Attendance during homeroom is what counts for the school to receive payment from the State for student attendance.

The end of the following semester was no different. Yet every year the principal would announce that we would be doing things a bit different in order to curtail school-wide chaos, improve student engagement, and ensure campus safety during finals. I realized that most teachers were okay with hearing the principal announce the "new plan" that would curtail the end of the semester chaos. The excitement would soon be overshadowed by the reality of year-end responsibilities.

After a couple of semesters teaching, I wondered why no one ever said anything about the hundreds of students that roamed the hallways after taking their finals. I wondered what taxpayers would say about the millions of dollars that are spent on maintaining schools open just to meet the state mandated number of days, despite the lack of instruction taking place after finals. Realistically it made no sense that students returned to class after taking their final exams. This is not the norm at the university level and it is impractical to expect students to attend class when no instruction takes place.

In 1999, I left the district to attend graduate school. I felt ill prepared to continue teaching. Eventually I would return to the classroom in 2002 at a different high school. The learning environment turned out to be worse. "The kids are nice," as so many colleagues eloquently stated, but the learning environment was a mode of survival. Like other low performing schools, there existed a handful of dedicated teachers who had clear objectives and a love for teaching, but most were indifferent.

After years of teaching with LAUSD, I decided that enough was enough. I could not continue to keep quiet and not say anything. Otherwise, I was just as guilty as everyone else on campus that saw what I saw and yet remained silent. I thought about journaling and publishing my experiences, but a combination of personal procrastination combined with the overwhelming workload made it a draining task. The following two years I spent my summers regretting not having kept a journal. I then realized that I should not be so hard on myself because the annual year-end chaos and everything else was guaranteed to repeat itself.

Finally, after years of witnessing much injustice and misuse of taxpayer dollars, as well as personally enduring constant harassment from administration, I decided to keep a journal of my experiences as a teacher. I rushed home every evening to write about the day. I played with several different formats until I realized I simply wanted to tell the story. So I began to write. Writing a story was like painting a portrait except I did not always have a clear picture in mind of the final product. Every sentence was like a brush stroke. I would work on small parts at a time, slowly shaping its form and defining its content.

My growing discontent for the district was the result of the strife and institutional racism that I experienced and that was interpreted as "my" misunderstanding. Regardless, students and parents were seldom heard. It pained me to see students come to class day in and day out, stressed out, tired, and frustrated. I also saw little to no academic growth in most of them during the course of a year. For most, their struggle would go in vain, for their reading, writing, or math skills were not improving. Every year the incoming class consisted of 1,300 ninth graders, only to have the number decline to approximately 550 by their senior year. At the end of their first year, the size of the entering class would decrease. It seemed like a symbolic inverted triangle. The same was true for the senior graduating class. At least twenty-five to thirty percent of the students who began in the fall would not complete the academic course by the spring. Yet administration did little to nothing to stop this never changing cycle. The following year consisted of more of the same. While the chaos continued, I saw seven administrators receive promotions within a five-year period. It baffled me to see administrators acknowledged and compensated without showing academic improvement and retention of their students.

Hence, I wrote this book because I truly believe that taxpayers are not aware of how their dollars are spent by the district. As we profess to be living in the best country in the world, how can students study in such deplorable conditions?

I was talking to a neighbor who happened to attend the same school where I was teaching. He shared that his ESL teacher would take the students out to play soccer for half of the two-hour instructional time. Had I not taught there I would have had a difficult time believing him. The reality is chilling. Students who barely speak English are

9

led to believe that they have a high school education. U.S. born students and native English speakers graduate with a ninth grade reading level and assume that they have a full and complete high school education. Parents do not know the difference and are proud of the ceremonial accomplishments.

I started this book after coming to terms that public schools have no real interest in educating all students. To educate all students would depreciate the value of a high school diploma within a capitalist system with its survival of the fittest mentality. Our society is structured to have a small number of rich people, with a big population of poor people. It coincides with education – there are a few well-educated people and many poorly educated ones. The origin of public education, as I am constantly reminded, was not built to prepare students for the university, but rather as a mandate to avoid child labor. This mandate keeps children from lowering the wages and taking jobs from adults. To understand the origins of public education makes it easier to understand why only eight out of one hundred Latinos and sixteen out of one hundred Blacks enrolled in kindergarten graduate from a four-year university. To understand the history of public education makes it easier to comprehend why so many Black male students have a better chance for recruitment to college through a sports program than through the regular admission's process.

Aside from all previously mentioned reasons, my greatest motivation for writing this book comes from the students themselves. The trust that formed between us with me as their teacher and mentor opened a door for them to confide in me. They have shared some of the most chilling and some of the most comical stories I have heard in my life. I have lost students to both gangs and cancer. I have had students get pregnant through consensual sex as well as rape. I have had students drop out of school because of work and/or because of teachers. I have been threatened with my life by a student. And I have been hugged and cried on for support. The students have organized more surprise birthday parties for me in my handful of years teaching than my family did during my childhood. They were the reason I stayed in the district this long. I have also been privileged to watch so many of them grow into their adulthood and settle into their professional careers. This experience was not absent of tears, frustration, laughter, hope, dancing and singing. The connection with students drives this work. Some students were not always ready to digest the material I would give and avoided taking my class altogether. Nevertheless, it has not failed that when I bump into a few of them every now and then, they express regret for not being disciplined enough to take my class.

It is 2007 and we are an advanced modern society thanks to the contributions of those who came before us. We should not settle for an outdated or second-hand education. We should not settle for an education system that has not been able to evolve with time; the industrial revolution is over. During the present state of the Information Age, students should have open access to information and it is time to retire the gatekeepers of our time.

I wrote this book based on the belief that it is my right to do so and as a part of living in a democracy. This is what I was encouraged to do while undergoing my studies in graduate school - to participate, create change, and not be a silent observer.

If Hallways Could Speak

If it were possible for school buildings to speak, what would they say? Where would they begin? Would they focus on the structure of the facility or on the experience of students who fill the overcrowded classrooms and hallways? What would the hallways say about your school and your personal experience? Would it disclose some personal secrets that you plan on taking to your grave? Would the hallways divulge the secret of the girl who got pregnant after school in the PE field under the bleachers? Or would they speak about the experience of a young student who smoked weed for the first time during his lunch break? What about the time wasted by students who sit in class with teachers with whom they have no real connection, never speaking a word - not even a "good morning" or "good afternoon?" Is it possible that the hallways would also ignore the experience of the masses and focus on the much smaller number of success stories?

The inspiration to write this essay came about during Spring 2006 when the school administrator, Ms. Acrimony, one of the six assistant principals at San Fernando High School (SFHS), was evaluating me. She walked into class during a student led service-learning project. The students had decided to focus on environmental racism and were looking at pictures and discussing which maps to use. Ms. Acrimony noticed that one of the photographs taken was of the school hallway and it displayed a huge hole that was approximately one and a half feet wide by two feet high. She immediately became defensive about the picture, as if the physical campus was well-maintained and supervised. To challenge her defensive attitude, I suggested to students that they take pictures of the blinds in the classroom and include them in their reports. Four of the seven blinds were broken and dangled like a paper fan. Only two of the seven windows opened. In a stronger defensive and accusatory tone, Ms. Acrimony then asked if I had submitted a request to get them repaired. "Yes, more than once," I replied. I thought to myself, "Should I have to file a request to repair the broken blinds, is it not obvious?" She made note of it and continued with her duties. The following period was my conference period at which point I reflected on Ms. Acrimony's visit. I remembered that the blinds were also broken in the room across the hall where I taught during the fall semester. I then wondered how long the blinds had been broken, and whether or not other teachers had reported the broken blinds. If the walls could speak, what story would they share about the blinds? Were the blinds broken by pissed off and mischievous students in reaction to something their teacher said or did? Or were they simply busted from regular wear and tear? I began to think of other secrets the walls of classrooms and hallways may be storing that are only remembered when alumni open their yearbooks.

I became intrigued by the secrets retained by the walls of classrooms and hallways. When the bell rings, the overwhelming majority of teachers at SFHS close their doors and only teachers and students know what really happens during the 61 minutes of instruction. While the overwhelming majority of doors are closed and administrators rarely walk the hallways, only the school building walls and the students strolling the hallways know what goes on outside during classroom hours. Only they would know who regularly burns the trashcans in the restroom or breaks the emergency fire alarms. Would the buildings abide by the code of silence that is so prevalent on the streets as well as in the school district? On the streets, everyone is expected to stay quiet and to tough it out. In the district, the attitude is slightly different. The code of silence with the district is "Don't ask, don't tell. If you are not happy, leave." Otherwise, the "don't ask, don't tell" policy is very much into effect. A perfect example of this policy is the murder of the young student at Venice High School who was shot in the teacher parking lot in June 2006. Only until a student was killed were the issues of school safety and need for security addressed. How is it possible that not one of the many adult employees was able to supervise? So, if no one loses an eye and if no parent complains why bother changing the status quo?

Have the buildings witnessed a rape or harassment? Did they see a student rape another student? Or did the walls witness a teacher harass a student or a student harass a teacher? I once assisted two young women in filing a sexual harassment report against a substitute teacher. The assistant principal (who is now a principal at another school) said she would investigate the matter. However, the girls were never interviewed about the incident and the substitute teacher continued to work. Other girls came forward but were discouraged to file a report after they witnessed the administrator's dismissive and apathetic behavior.

If walls could speak, they would mention the inconsistent enforcement of school policy. They witnessed a student walkout in 2006. The following day the deans summoned student protestors from class and cited them with a truancy ticket. Yet, students who were ditching for days or weeks were not cited. This is an inexplicable injustice. What would parents say if they found out that their children were cited for exercising their constitutional right, while the students who were not attending school for other reasons were not? This double standard could be interpreted as a violation of the educational code, which gives schools the right to cite a student for ditching. If the school, as was the case with San Fernando High School, does not ticket chronic ditchers and focuses on student protestors, is that not evidence of unjust application of school policy? The parents of the ditchers should also be upset with the fact that their children are being neglected.

I return to the original question, if hallways could speak what would they say? Would they mention the lack of respect that exists within the education system and is tolerated in schools? I hear the constant verbal disrespect between students as they easily call each other "nigga," "bitch," "ho," "*buey,*" "*cabron,*" "*hijo de la chingada,*" "*hijo de puta,*" "*mammon.*" These names, or verbal assaults, are so common in the hallways that we are desensitized to their vulgarity. A blatant lack of respect also exists between student and teacher. Would the hallways shed light on the school's internal profile of students that would shock parents? What would they say about young couples who make out soft-porn style between bungalows (temporary buildings), hallways, inside classrooms, behind bushes, and any other hidden corner on campus? It is commonplace to see a couple grinding each other while waiting for class to begin. What else do buildings see during these make-out sessions that faculty do not? What is the motive for these make-out sessions? Is it their youthful curiosity or their need to feel the affection they seldom get at home or elsewhere?

Too often, the silence of the walls reflects the silence of the general student body. I often wish that the walls could speak in order to support student claims. "Why speak if no one cares?" is a sentiment expressed by so many students. I encourage them to speak to the Principal or to write a letter to Administration, but they feel discouraged. Too many students are accustomed to not being heard by their parents, teachers, or other adults. Thus, they have learned to live in silence. It is a silence that fills the room when I pose a question. More difficult than answering a question is posing one, and the majority of the students struggle to do either.

If the walls could speak, would they tell us about the students' secrets? Would they share the many stories of broken hearts, false promises, casualties of gang warfare, drug use and abuse, loneliness, or the thought of suicide, and everything else that chips away at the innocence of these young human beings? What happened to the young student who promised eternal love in exchange for a young's woman first sexual experience? Were the walls witnesses to how it all began? The flirting that started in class or maybe in the cafeteria line? Or witnessing the notes passed between them in the hallway, or through a mutual friend? It was so beautiful and innocent when it all began. Now she cannot focus in class, feeling like she was played. Disappointed with love, she sits in class distracted wondering if a man will ever love her again – as if the first one ever did – for not being a virgin. Her mother's words echo in her thoughts and the image of her mother cannot be erased from her mind. The feelings of guilt and shame overshadow the importance of the class discussion. What would her mother think of her now? If only the guy would understand that someone will also one day play with his sister and or daughter, just as he has done with someone else, will this game of false promises end? As quickly as he made himself forget the last one, the romancing of the next young woman begins. Girls know he is a player, yet they seemed to think that they could be the one to change his ways. If only the walls could speak, they would explain that the sexual game is old and has been happening since time began.

I wonder if the walls were witnesses to the disagreement that led to a shooting between two gangs. Who would tell the story behind the t-shirts that so many students wear with R.I.P. adorned on the back? There was a time when I was attending a funeral approximately every six months. I never cared to buy a sweater or a t-shirt, but I know people who ordered one for every death. As I watched one person after another walk in my classroom with the sweater, I wondered how many people would wear a sweater for my funeral. As a teenager, I attended so many funerals that I would imagine myself inside the casket and wondered how many people would show up. Would the homeboys be taking group pictures next to my casket, as we had done with others? Today as much as I attempt to disconnect personal feelings, I cringe with pain and agony when I see students walking around with sweaters or shirts that have a big R.I.P. on the back, with the name and sometimes picture of the deceased. The story and symbolism of the sweater usually paints the dead teen as an innocent victim, but the cause of death is not always known. Was it an act of revenge for someone else's death or did someone take the gang turf too seriously? Maybe it is me who is passing judgment on the students as well as on the deceased being honored on a sweater. Maybe the death had nothing to do with gangs at all...

At this point, we still do not know the capacity of the walls or the secrets they keep. Would the walls be able to identify the soft and subtle racism that is so deeply rooted in our society? Some of the racism is within the paper of our textbooks. It is for this reason that books such as Howard Zinn's *The People's History of the United States: 1492 to Present* and James Loewen's *Lies My Teacher Told Me* seem to contradict what we learned in traditional textbooks. The contradiction is so profound that some students find the information hard to believe. These books challenge a knowledge that most students (middle school, high school, and even college) have accepted as true, depending on their professor, of course.

Would the hallways be able to attest to the beginnings of this "life sentence" that is so real on campus where millions of young students across the nation are discouraged from being bilingual and feel ashamed for being a non-English native speaker; or have a name in any language other than English? Entire families spend more money on hair products to look white than what they would be willing to spend on college books. The media and the moneymaking corporations have us believing it is fashion. Families give English names to their children they cannot spell or pronounce, further adding to the shame of being different. Yet everywhere else in the world people celebrate bilingualism and multiculturalism.

Although the walls cannot speak, there are some obvious things to us all. The general practice of low expectations is killing the Black and Brown communities. According to statistics, sixteen out of one hundred Black kindergarten students obtain a four-year degree. For Chicanos and Latinos only eight out of one hundred obtain a four-year degree. It is obvious that in some major universities a good percentage of the Black student population are athletes. It is impossible to find a college football or basketball team that does not have a Black athlete, yet there are too many doctoral programs that do not have a single Black student. Although Chicanos and Latinos are expected to be the largest minority group and exceed a certain population number by 2050, there are countless university departments where they have yet to graduate their first Chicano or Latino student. This is an obvious fact that does not need to be confirmed by inside knowledge of classroom walls. Too often counselors and teachers will say, "College is not for everyone." Aside from the fact that their job is to encourage students to excel in school, this statement is most likely nonexistent at Beverly Hills High School or even within Advanced Placement (AP) courses. Teachers and counselors alike would be reprimanded on the spot for making such a discouraging statement. In a videotaped interview, a counselor from Project Grad was asked if all students from San Fernando High School were being prepared to go to college. He stated, "The reality is that not everyone is meant to go to college, we need mechanics and cooks." It is obvious that we need mechanics and cooks, but that should be the choice of an educated student, and not the choice of an academic counselor who is advising a student who has a difficult time reading the newspaper.

Do the hallways at different schools share the same experiences? Would they share war stories to see which wall has seen worse? Do they house the same number of police officers, security screens, and security dogs?

Is it possible that the hallways witness the frustration of the thousands of students who day in and day out wake up early for school with the expectation of learning something new, yet arrive to that same monotonous learning environment from the day before? What happens to the thousands of students who want a better life and look to the experts for guidance yet are asked to settle for something a lot less challenging? Assistant Principal Ms. Acrimony encouraged me to give a student make-up homework; the student had thirty missing assignments and twenty-five absences. It was not the first or the last time that Ms. Acrimony would make that type of request in front of parents. I stood my ground and refused the request. What would the student learn from completing a pile of assignments? How does this prepare them for college? Why are the school districts not taking any responsibility for the low expectations that are contributing to the low enrollment at major universities? Is it possible that the high schools could admit that they exploit the skills of young Black males in football and basketball and admit how little they prepare these young athletes academically? I have seen many coaches and a few parents mislead young bright athletes. So much importance is given to sports that they are willing to settle for the minimum GPA of 2.0, which is not good enough for any university. Many of these athletes go straight to the community college and do not transfer out to obtain a four-year degree. I witnessed this revolving door first person as an athlete and now as a teacher. What is to become of so many young adults who are led to believe that they have graduated from high school, despite reading below a ninth grade level. I once had a former student visit me. She was crying as she talked about not testing at the college level English, despite taking Honors English courses in high school. What would the hallways say about that? Is an honors class at San Fernando High School the same as an honors class at Beverly Hills High School? I do not know. If only the walls could speak…

Fight on Campus

There is never a dull day at San Fernando High School. Everyday is so different from the day before, yet ironically, everyday is more of the same. Today, as I sat back in a recliner that I have in my classroom, preparing to eat my lunch, I heard a scuffle in the hallway. My thoughts automatically imagined a group of restless students horse-playing in the hallway. The noise got louder and louder. Just as I warmed the enchiladas, one of my favorite dishes, I realized that the scuffle was in fact a fight. Two male students figured they could go upstairs inside the two-story building and handle their business. Their need to beat the living daylights out of each other was so intense that no one, spectators included, gave any attention to the fact the door from my room was open. Over the years, I have busted plenty of students with drugs, tagging, fighting, and making out that students who are up to no good tend to avoid me.

As soon as I realized that it was a brawl, I dropped everything on my desk and ran out the door. As I pushed my door shut to avoid it staying slightly open, I was able to see from the corner of my eye that one of them was already on the floor. I felt his desperation to get up, but it would have been a difficult thing to do. His rival was a bit taller and was directly over him. My first clear shot was of the guy on top, who wore a long sleeve yellow shirt. He jumped over his opponent who was already on the floor and swung with his right as he leaped to better position himself. Everyone who surrounded the fighters cheered them on, not thinking of the consequences. Their excitement reminded me of the popular, but brutal cockfights that I have seen so many times in Mexico. Like the cocks in a fight, both students seemed determined to take each other out until death of the other was achieved.

The minute I ran down the hallway, a student recognized me and immediately yelled, "El Maestro!" (the teacher). The crowd quickly scattered and attempted to run out the building. The student in the yellow shirt was not able to complete his last blow, as he stumbled over his opponent to flee from the scene of the crime. The one on the bottom got up and dusted himself so quick that he seemed to forget how bad he was getting his ass kicked a few seconds before. It was a hilarious sight, but I had no time to laugh, I was on a mission to catch them both. It was amazing to witness the confusion in the hallway, as everyone ran in every direction to exit the building. Some students seem to be running in circles, while others were literally running into each other, and some just ran in place. They ran, or at least they felt like they were running, as "El Maestro" rapidly approached the scene of the crime. The hysteria got bigger as I approached. By the time I arrived to the area where both students were tangled in what could have easily turned into a life-threatening match, most of the students were running down the stairs. They attempted to block me from pursuing the two *gallos*, or roosters, but I was too determined to catch them. I began to force my way through the crowd. Some of the students got a kick out of seeing my determination, while others seemed to be surprised at how easily I was able to push them out of the way. Forgetting that they were cheering on for the ultimate defeat in a fight just seconds earlier, they seemed to be expecting me to mind my manners and say excuse me. Their eyes widened as I pushed them left and right with backpacks and all. Some began to express their discomfort, but I ran by them so fast that they did not have a chance to voice their concerns.

As I ran down the stairs, I skipped some of the stairs and double stepped in others. I finally made it to the bottom. I leaped over three or four steps before landing the last set of stairs. I did not realize it at the time but I was following yellow-shirt. I never really knew what the other one looked like. I only saw him throw his arms and legs in the air, as he desperately attempted to get up. As I approached him, I noticed that he did not run outside. I immediately looked to my right and found my target. I began to run and could already feel his shoulders on my fingertips, just as I also realized that I was still attempting to balance myself. I attempted to pick up speed and balance myself simultaneously. I bobbled to my left, then to my right as I looked in front of me so I would not lose sight of yellow-shirt. With so many outsiders and former students entering the campus on a regular basis, I was not sure if he was one of our students. I maintained pursuit and remained focused on my target. Just as I attempted to shift myself into fourth gear, I picked up distance as my body plummeted a few yards in front of my original position and landed on my knees. Damn that hurt! Both the palm of my hands and knees were stinging. What stung even more was hearing the cheering squad break into extreme laughter. I suppose to a student, nothing can be funnier than seeing a teacher fly a few yards and land in the most abrupt way. I wanted to turn around and say something, but I did not have time. For a split second, I also thought of calling it quits, but I could not do that. If anything, I am always telling my students not to give up. I got up and continued with my pursuit. I knew that I would have to work a lot harder to catch up. I began to reach for my cell phone to call campus security, but then remembered what a slow response we have from them. I let go of the phone in my pocket and concentrated on catching up to yellow-shirt. As I ran down the hallway, I saw that he was exiting the building. I was not expecting any student to help me and knew that I would have to catch him myself. As I ran I looked for other adults in the area, but no one was available. They were in the faculty cafeteria or inside their rooms with their doors completely shut. Tuning out the hysteria in the hallway, none of them had a clue as to what was happening. If they did have a clue, they wanted no part of it. As I ran out the building past the doors, a couple who was making out, before the commotion started, took a breather from swapping saliva and watched me run by. They were regulars in that spot. The guy, in his most nonchalant tone, casually said, "hey Gutierrez." I wanted to laugh in disbelief at the surreal situation. Here I was in pursuit of one student who was brawling while another student was on cloud nine from his daily lunchtime kissing marathon with his high school sweetheart. I remember replying with a simple "What's up?" But it really didn't matter at the time; I was on a mission to catch the brawler. Suddenly, he ran around the next building, known as the Tiger Building, and disappeared from my view. I identified some of his cheerleading squad, who served as the trail of crumbs I needed. Wherever I saw a large group of them, I knew he was there. As I continued to run alongside the Tiger Building, one of his friends made eye contact with me. Without saying a word, he challenged me with his eye contact. It is amazing how much he told me without ever saying a word. By now I was on "street mode" and was using any and all of my streets smarts to accomplish my mission. Without my having to utter a word, I accepted his challenge. Like a hawk, I honed in on my target. This friend attempted to confuse me by looking in a different direction, and pretending that was where my target was running. I did not buy it, and could sense him to be a lot closer. I slowed down my pace and began to walk as I approached the friend. The friend did not realize it, but he had already told me everything through our eye contact. I said nothing to the friend and walked right into the classroom with the door open. There the student stood by the door in absolute silence. When I walked in, yellow-shirt took a final sigh, as if to say, "I'm done running" then looked up as if to say, "God, why did you let him catch me?" I did not have to say anything to him; he walked in my direction with the "take me away" attitude. The teacher in the classroom did not say anything either and was as wide-eyed as were the students who were scrambling to make it out of the building minutes earlier. As we walked towards the Dean's Office, I looked in every direction for adult supervision. No one was visible. I started to think that there was a faculty party to which I was not invited. As we walked across campus, many of the students who saw what had happened were communicating silently through the expression in their eyes. Some were wide-eyed in disbelief of me being able to catch him, while others nodded and showed a high level of respect, never doubting, and knowing that I am not one to give up. A small handful of them simply said, "hey Gutierrez" while others expressed fear that they too were going to get busted for being accomplices in the ugly brawl. The more we walked toward the Dean's Office the more I began to feel the throbbing pulse on both of my knees from the fall. With all of the past sports injuries to my knees, I could not wait to check them out. I finally found one of the six assistant principals, told him the story, handed yellow-shirt over and returned to class.

As I walked back to my classroom, I was scouting the area for the other student. I did not know what he looked like, but I knew that the students were being transparent in trying to be nonchalant and hide him. I was also having a difficult time catching my breath, but my posture was composed. I began to cough a lot, and my throat felt raspy. As I past by the group of male students who were cheering on the fighters, they stayed quiet. Many continued to talk to me through the expression of their eyes. A few apologized for participating in that fiasco, but most were terrified that they too would possibly be getting in trouble. Before I walked up the stairs, I decided to check the boys' restroom. As I was walking in, another male teacher was also by the door. We both walked and the second we entered, two boys suspiciously cut their conversation and quickly walked into different stalls. I asked the other teacher to guard the door, so that no one would run out. At least that is what I wanted to happen, but I am not sure that I was explicit enough. I was still out of breath, and the pain in my knees was intensifying. I continued with my search. It appeared that both of the students who walked into the stalls were in the middle of a transaction or at least I suspected so because of their demeanor. I did not see anything and I knew that there were no adults outside who could assist me in the process of searching them. I gently kicked open the door in the stalls to ensure that nothing inappropriate or illegal was actually happening. Neither one of them was the guy I was following, nor did I have the energy to begin a new investigation, so we left.

As my colleague and I walked up the stairs, he shared that he had heard the raucous - after all, it did happen right outside of his classroom. He shared how he was in his room with his legs resting on top of his desk when the fight began. By the time he sat up and went outside, the hallway was empty. As we walked up the stairs and I listened to his story, I began to wonder how many other teachers heard the fight and chose not to come outside.

I began to settle back into the reality of my everyday school experience, one where most adults have no real connection with students. Few teachers interact with students outside of the mandated hour of instruction.

I returned to my classroom and picked up where I left off. I picked up my homemade enchiladas and headed to the classroom across the hall where a colleague allowed me to use her microwave. She expressed that a few minutes earlier, a group of students were screaming at the other end of the hallway. "It was a fight," I explained. In the usual blasé tone of an "Oh" was all that she replied.

Self-Sabotage

Every week I see young students afraid of their own power and intelligence. Their fears keep them from envisioning success, wealth, and everything else that can alter their current living situation.

Day in and day out, I see some students struggle to do well in class even though they are the smartest students I have ever met. Unfortunately, they use their intelligence in other ways like getting themselves out of trouble or thinking of great stories to tell their mothers, fathers, judges, teachers, counselors, probation officers, or cops. I can think of dozens of students who every semester attend class, sit quietly, absorb every word I speak and understand the concepts being taught. Yet they do nothing with the knowledge they gain. Some of them are in graffiti tagging crews or gangs, while others belong to a small group of friends who support their rebellious attitude. Some of these students attempt to turn their life around when they turn 18 and then are hit with the reality of adulthood. However, their delayed interest in taking care of business is not enough for them to graduate with their class. They finally have reached a level of maturity where they understand the consequences of their actions and wrongdoing. Unfortunately, they finish their senior year without having enough credits to graduate. Others get an early wake-up call and literally surprise their family and friends by graduating and picking up their diploma on stage. Those students have beat the odds by barely squeezing by, but have set up this unfortunate "start" to their life after high school. Many of these students were told by several teachers and counselors, even some parents, that they would not graduate: that they were losers and or bums. Yet their determination to prove people wrong is what drove them to graduate on stage. They are the ones who bring tears to my eyes on graduation day. Their surprise and excitement to cross the stage is visible from afar. They often want to say thank you, but do not have the words to do so. Their watery eyes speak for themselves. To say a word would run the risk of them being vulnerable and breaking down emotionally, which is not going to happen in a public place with hundreds of people standing around. The genuine emotion in their eyes says it all, and it is more than I would have been able to express at their age. At times, the connection is so strong between us that I avoid them all together for fear of also being vulnerable and showing too many emotions in public. I suppose the student learned well from the teacher.

For those that sabotage their chance of getting to that place – the glorious stage on graduation day, their fears are many and real. They are afraid of what they do not know, and perceive any form of achievement to be an impossible task. They are afraid of success, making a lot of money, wearing a suit and tie to work, having a college degree, having unforeseen power, and anything else that would completely alter their current living situation. Basically, they are scared of change, and naturally, the unknown. Let's face it, in general, the public school system is a joke. Passing the classes is not difficult, but succeeding academically is another story. Anyone who wants to graduate can do so. This is not difficult to admit, despite being a teacher within the public school system. A bit more difficult is returning to work everyday knowing that I am part of the system, designed to fail many students and that such a lax and inept environment makes it easier for students to sabotage their future.

For the love of life, I cannot understand why so many students fail. Some of them go to school everyday, sit, and do nothing. It is as if their journey through life had removed their spirit and only flesh and bones walked on earth. Most of them are nice and respectful, but their attitude is not enough to pass the class nor is it a prerequisite. A handful of them constantly challenge me, not because they want to learn, but instead question me to see how well I know the material. They challenge hoping to make an example of me and disrupt the learning environment. Worst of all, they challenge me to avoid being responsible for their own actions. I once had a couple of students who would enter class thirty minutes late on a regular basis. Their excuses were pathetic: "my locker got stuck," "I had to go to the bathroom," "I couldn't find my book," or "I walked my friend to class." They would do anything to disrupt the class and make their classmates laugh. What neither one of them understood was that I once had been in their shoes. Not one of them was as bad as I had been, yet unlike me, they consistently failed most of their classes. I attempted to understand their come-from in order to modify my response to their actions. As much as I tried to understand them and thought I could because of our similar experiences, I could not.

Having been a rebellious student myself, the king of ditching parties, and having participated in occasional fights, I still managed to pass all of my classes and graduate on time. Somehow, I also managed to be eligible to play sports, except for the time that I was suspended from three games for trespassing on a neighboring school. I needed to cash a debt with a handful of guys who had jumped my younger brother the week before. That incident was a reality check for me. First, my brother was jumped in a way that I could not imagine. According to eyewitnesses, a group of about seven to eight guys, a couple of them twice as old as him, beat him to the ground and repeatedly kicked him while others broke bottles over his head. I first heard of the incident from a homeboy after a school football game. I immediately thought the worst. I also thought of my parents and having to explain the unexplainable. Where would I begin? I thought of my brother and began to imagine every possible outcome to the beating. I began to remember when I would go home and share with him what was happening at the junior high, making the war stories seem like something fun. I remembered how intelligent he was, always taking honors and other advanced courses, and the fact that he did not belong in that environment. I began to experience a wave of conflicting emotions about the brutal beating he endured. Before I felt any rage towards the perpetrators, I experienced a great deal of compassion for my brother and felt guilty for having introduced him to the gang, also referred to as the neighborhood. In a weird way, he was already there and needed no introduction as we lived in the belly of the beast. Within moments, I began to premeditate my revenge. I calculated every step. My thoughts were sick and only continued to fill every inch of my body with rage. My premeditated thoughts, however, began and ended in my mind. I knew that carrying out my violent vision would cross a line that I would later regret. As it was, I felt trapped within a neighborhood that did not belong to me. To cross the line would mean to be a lifer in the hood, and I knew that was not for me.

I called home and asked for my brother. My parents were oblivious to what had happened hours before. They told me he was not home and was working. I felt like a ton of bricks had been lifted off my chest. No news is better than bad news, I thought to myself. However, within the small boundaries of the neighborhood news travels fast. I figured that my parents not knowing meant that my brother was okay. Later that night when he finally arrived home from work, the beating he took hours earlier was not noticeable, miraculously. Apparently, a friend who was not even from the neighborhood jumped in and managed to single-handedly tackle the guys off my brother. Then a group of classmates pulled him into a car and drove away. I do not know how the other guy did it, but he managed to get away untouched. This happened on a Friday and I had the entire weekend to rally the troops.

When Monday came around, three or four of us went to the junior high school that my brother attended and took care of business during nutrition and lunch. The feud was on. The rumor was that everything would be resolved after school, with the expectation that both sides would have a lot of reinforcement. By the end of sixth period, several cars filled with guys were roaming the school and ready to rumble. The bulk of my homeboys were nowhere in sight. Only two or three showed up. Seeing that most of my homeboys were not there to back us up was the second biggest lesson of this whole incident. "Fuck it! We will handle it however we have to," I said to myself. However, there were too many of them and it would have been suicidal to stand there and fight. We were outnumbered four to one. They ran out of their cars with bats and pipes. We had nothing. Some guys looked as old as my dad. They appeared to have just been released from the penitentiary bearing their old jailhouse tats. Yet they were fighting with teenagers over a street or neighborhood that they did not own. Some of them had *Brown Pride* tattooed on their arms and or necks. I began to wonder how older men with tattoos of *Brown Pride* could be there to beat up on boys half their age who were also brown.

Short of a miracle, it was a good thing that no one was seriously hurt that afternoon. As far as I can recall only the school police officer was struck by a metal pipe across his legs. The blow was intended for me, but the officer jumped in between and did not see the pipe in motion. The P.E. coach recognized me and called the high school. I was suspended from school and could not play for the remainder of the football season. I was pissed off! I had worked hard enough to be the only one from my homeboys to make it on the football team my first year in high school. I still had to show up to practice and to all of the games. It was torture.

My homeboys began to dropout of high school and were leaving me alone in a hostile environment. Worse, most of them were not there to back me up when I needed them. That was a reality check. I had to learn to fend for myself and to travel the journey of life alone.

Despite going through all this, I never failed a class in high school. So it's difficult for me to understand why so many of my students fail. When I ask them why, most of them cannot explain. It is as if they are shocked by what society expects of them. The students who attempt to disrupt my class know nothing of my past and think that I do not understand the game they are playing. They seem to think that they invented ditching and screwing around. They seem to think that I must have grown up elsewhere and do not understand the unwritten rules of a "ghetto" school, a term used by so many students to refer to SFHS. Only a few students continue to challenge me, and those who do quickly discover that I also "play" the hard way. The majority understand that my message is positive and practical. In addition, they also learn quickly that I am a no nonsense type of teacher. They learn that I have strong intuition, common sense, and the courage to visit their homes or call their parents.

Years after I left the neighborhood, I had a conversation with a homeboy who had just finished doing time. He was telling me about how bad things were getting in the neighborhood. He went on to tell me that life in the hood was difficult. He shared some of the sad stories that were part of the everyday life: youngsters wounded in the street wars, killed, pregnant, or in prison. Their little brothers and sisters would join the ranks and also sell and/or use crack. In essence, it continued to be a life of violence, drugs, and sex. I could not stop thinking of those who were incarcerated for long periods of time. As much as I tried to place myself in their shoes, I could not understand why they would not avoid going to the extreme. Of course, I too did things that would have put me in jail had I been caught, but I never felt the need to go to the extreme and risk doing serious time. I tried explaining to him that life outside of the neighborhood was not so easy. I shared with him my difficulties attending college and being in a predominantly white environment. As I listened to his stories, I realized that both places were difficult for different reasons, respectively. Surely being shot at or living in fear of being caught in public by a group of enemies was no way to live. However, he knew little of what it was like to sit in class alone and feel marginalized, with no back up whatsoever, and engage in a discussion with White students who had a different upbringing.

At that point in time my homeboy could not understand the difficulty of sitting next to white students who blatantly offended me with their subtle racist comments. To me, this experience was a lot harder than staying in the neighborhood where few of us disagreed. In the neighborhood major disagreements were handled in the parking lot of apartment buildings, at the park, in back of grocery stores, in grassy areas, or right on the spot! In college, disagreements were settled by the use of words.

There were no parking lots, no discretion; it happened right in front of the entire class. In many ways, for someone like me who had a limited vocabulary, *duking it* out in class was more intimidating than going to a parking lot. Initially, I had a better chance in a parking lot brawl than in a college class discussion.

I eventually learned how to defend myself with words and saw the classroom as a boxing ring. It was a place where two or more people handled their differences with the use of words and discussions and not by physical contact. Unlike the neighborhood, where there was a winner and a loser, the class discussions did not always have a clear winner or loser.

Initially my limited vocabulary led to major frustrations. I often wanted to stand up and walk right out of the discussion. "Fuck this shit! What do they know?" I would say to myself. Nevertheless, I stayed and was determined to learn how to defend myself in that arena. I had recently read Malcolm X's autobiography and could identify with his struggle on education. Like Malcolm, I slowly discovered the power of words and their meaning. As difficult as it was, I needed to keep moving forward.

Going to college was like being in an ESL program all over again. Every level of college was like an advanced version of English and I always felt like I was behind everyone. Despite passing my classes in college and receiving positive comments from professors, I continued to carry a negative self-image. It was like swimming through the rough waves of the ocean. But I could not go back to where I came from, so I kept swimming.

Maybe this is what students feared – the ability to swim in the ocean when they are only accustomed to wading by the shore. I am not sure of their exact fears and I do not think that they are aware of them either. One thing is certain. Too many students latch onto their school and are afraid to face the world. Are they aware of their (mandatory) promotion in grade levels in public schools and feel ill prepared to face the world? Or are they stuck in a purgatory state, not wanting what their parents had, yet afraid of not knowing how to step out of their box and create something different? For the students who are absent two to three days per week (and always absent on the day of the test) is this a safe way to ensure that they fail so they could buy time to grow up? One thing is certain, failing a test or class is not an option. So rather than risk failing the test, they just avoid taking it altogether. Technically, in their mind they do not fail.

What does this say about all of the stakeholders within the educational system and their contribution to the problem of self-sabotage? Every one of the stakeholders points in a different direction, refusing to accept responsibility and be accountable for their actions or lack thereof. Parents blame teachers and administrators, and neglect to see their disconnection to the schools and their children. School administrators are afraid of parents and want teachers and students to be accountable but neglect to see their negligence as a whole, giving too much importance to standardized tests that do not count towards graduation. Students will point to teachers, administrators and sometimes parents, but neglect to see their apathetic attitude. Policy makers want to hold teachers and administrators accountable, but are too blind to see their lack of experience and meaningless expectations, focusing on the superficiality of test scores. Higher-level administrators want to please policy makers, they tend to make excuses for parents and focus on school administration and teachers, forgetting what it was like to be in the classroom and deal with the district bureaucracy. Education, in a huge district like LAUSD, has become a game of survival in an arena where everyone wants to protect their job, but who is protecting the students?

Teaching at My Alma Mater

Monroe High School, my alma mater, was the school where I began my first teaching assignment. Initially I welcomed the assignment with great enthusiasm. As it turned out the experience was extremely rewarding, despite having to confront the ghosts from the past. As I walked through the hallways, my ghost became my shadow and walked by my side everyday. At times, I would get nostalgic of distant memories. Some of these memories were beautiful and reminded me of my ex-girlfriends. Other memories were hilarious and reminded me of the days when I would clown around. How could I not remember some of the many secrets of the hallways, where students were threatened or fights took place? These were secrets that the hallways did a good job of not sharing with others. I remembered one fight in the boys bathroom in G Hall. The art teacher stood and watched at least thirty guys go into the bathroom and allowed us to fight. He then pretended to care and asked us all to disperse. As he asked everyone to leave campus, he was chuckling with amusement. I never believed that his screws were tight and occasionally wondered how he became a teacher.

The more I walked the hallways the more that I was confronted by the ghost from the past. I was temporarily surprised to see the younger brothers and sisters of some of my homeboys. It was a shock to us both. Some of these younger siblings knew me very well while others had never met me before. The ones who new me well seem to only remember the dumb things I did as a teenager. Although my past was my past and I was not embarrassed, nor proud of it – it was what it was – it did however become a problem when they shared my past with their friends. It made me nervous to think that the general student body would know my past. Far worse, I feared that students, who were members of my once rival gang, would hold my past against me and not participate in class. *Dicho y hecho*, students found out about my old gang affiliations and a handful of them refused to take my class. They disrespected me as a teacher. For a small handful, the continued war on the streets made it difficult for them to make the distinction between my past and the present. The occasional updates from my students kept me informed of the never-ending street wars. Because of my new role as a teacher, these updates always gave me conflicting emotions. I was torn to hear that one of my homeboys had been shot. I was equally as torn to hear that members of my old neighborhood were harassing my students in the hallways and/or on the streets. I did not have an answer for my students when I heard that members of my old neighborhood wanted to control campus as if it were the streets. What did this mean for me? Should I take a side? Do I defend my students? Alternatively, do I play a role and allow my homeboys an entry to the school? I realized then that I was no longer a gang member and that upset many of my own homeboys. A few understood that I had a job to do as a teacher and did not take it personal. Others became angry and called me to a meeting, which I refused to attend.

At times teaching was a bit overwhelming. I never thought that my past could become part of my present. One of my worst memories is of an incident that took place minutes after the final bell rang. As I walked to my car a *ghetto-bird* (a patrolling helicopter) flew over the school and stopped right over the southeast corner of the football field. A friend, who was observing my class for the day, casually asked me what had happened. In my mind I replied, "How am I to know if we both walked out of the same building." I jokingly stated, "Who knows...someone probably got shot." Shootings were so common in the area that my statement was only half jokingly, but very likely. I later found out that as the crowd of students waited at the intersection, two members of my old neighborhood, one was a former student in my class, drove up on a bike and with a shotgun fired at the entire crowd of students who were waiting to cross the intersection. Three students were injured, none of whom were members of any gang. Fortunately, it was a sawed-off shotgun, and his anxiety to pull the trigger got the best of him. He shot from a long enough of a distance that only individual pellets, not enough to do any serious physical harm, penetrated the bodies of the injured students. At least that is the story that I got from students the next day.

I was filled with mixed emotions. I experienced anger as well as compassion for the guy who pulled the trigger. I was angry for what he had done. But I had compassion for what he did to himself. Homeboys were already over-represented in prisons. We did not need one more to go to prison. I also felt guilt and shame for having been part of the birth of that gang. Students would occasionally ask if my affiliation was true. Some asked, hoping that I would say no. I could see their face fill with disappointment the minute I confessed. Their face of disappointment only added to my guilt.

In time, the majority of the students learned to make the distinction between my past and present. I suppose my honesty made things easier for them to accept that I too was young and rebellious at one point. Personally, dealing with the ghost from the past was not always easy. One day, while walking through my classroom aisles to supervise a test I noticed a family picture inside the plastic cover of the folder belonging to a student. I focused enough to recognize the face of a couple of guys with whom I went to school. Although we grew up in different neighborhoods and ran with rival gangs, we managed to respect each other.

In that moment of seeing the picture, I remembered an incident that occurred during my senior year in high school. I was standing in front of the campus appreciating the sights, the girls, and the cars during cruising hours. As I stood there, a car full of members from a rival gang pulled up. I locked eyes with the first one that I recognized, then with another, and another. Eventually I locked eyes and identified every single one of them, and they had already identified me as well. I could see and feel their rage. I said nothing. I simply continued to carefully monitor every move they made. I was also careful not to make any sudden moves that would make them react. It was a tense moment. The air began to feel thick. Everyone else seemed to be having a good time. During the time of the incident I was no longer involved with my neighborhood gang, but my past could not be easily erased and my rage for them still ran through my veins, for they had tried more than once to take my life, and had succeeded one time too many on a couple of my homeboys. I was scared but could not show it. I reflected the same anger and determination that they carried. Otherwise, they would take full advantage of any perceived weakness. Despite distancing myself from the neighborhood, there was no way that I would show fear or weakness. I raised my chin to my confidence and pride, even though internally I was terrified. I thought of my homeboys who seemed to think that I was no longer caught up in the mix. They thought that my problems ended the day my family moved from the neighborhood and I stopped hanging out. Boy, were they wrong! Contrary to what they believed, all of the shootings and violence of the neighborhood still affected me. I continued to look over my shoulder as if I still lived and kicked it there. Enemies made no distinction or cared who was active and who had settled down. They only made associations, and once they associated you with a gang, it was on.

This vivid memory ran through my mind in a matter of seconds as I looked at the picture that my student had on her folder. The ghost from the past was with me once more.

It did not seem like they were expecting to bump into anyone. At that particular moment they were not ready to do anything. I carefully glanced around through the corner of my eye to scope out the entire area, yet never taking my eyes off them. I could tell the passenger wanted to shout something, but did not. More than anything, I sensed a certain level of excitement from having caught me alone. He stared me down in silence, as if to declare a checkmate! As much as I wanted to yell "check" at him, I knew better.

Since they were not prepared to do anything, the driver stepped on the gas and went to make a u-turn one hundred feet ahead. A car behind followed. I was in shock and had frozen, not knowing what was about to happen. Because of the cruising, their u-turn was not so easy. I began to recover from the state of shock, and looked around for the guys I was kicking it with. No one was packing (a weapon) that day. Worse yet, none of them were in sight. I remembered they went to get the car. I was alone facing two cars filled with guys who clearly wanted to violently remove the life right out of my body. It was clear that they had no regard for my family or the consequences of killing me.

As they pulled up in front of me for the second time, I stood there expecting them to get out and rush me. It did not happen. Instead, the back seat window began to roll down slowly. I could not see anyone. The tinted windows made it impossible. Within seconds, a long double barrel shot gun began to creep its way out of the back seat. Still I could not see anyone and I suddenly did not know what to do. I looked in one direction then the other hoping my homeboys would pull up. There was no such luck! No one was around to save me! In that moment, I wished that I were still in the neighborhood to have the needed support to deal with these knuckleheads. Instead, I was by myself in the middle of cruising where few people knew me and those who did wanted to kill me. The barrels were long, and the guy who would pull the trigger struggled to get it out from the back seat. I thought of running, but did not. I ran long enough and was tired. It goes without mentioning that I would have looked like a bitch had I ran. I also caught myself thinking that the shooter was an idiot for not being able to quickly draw and shoot. I thought too soon! What seemed like a split second, the window was low enough for him to straighten it out and aim at his target. The driver of the car behind them noticed what was unfolding and pulled up beside them, blocking them from having a clear shot. The driver was Jose. He is in the family photo that triggered this memory. Even though they were his homeboys, he saved my life. He knew that I was no longer involved and that I was determined to graduate from high school. I could hear him yell, attempting to convince his homeboys that I was no longer active. I stood there waiting for a different reaction, as if Jose's story of my determination to graduate from school would remove the rage that ran through their veins. The reality was different, they did not care that I was determined to graduate they only wanted to pay back a debt to my old neighborhood. It did not matter whose life cashed the debt, as long as it was cashed. Moreover, it was a bigger payoff to get someone who was on the path of straightening out his life. All casualties hurt, but when someone who is innocent, doing well, or a parent goes down, the casualty seems to hurt a little more. All of the guys in both cars were at the right place and time, and were salivating a victory for their neighborhood.

The driver sped up to clear the shot, but Jose was determined to continue blocking it with his car. The driver then took off and attempted to make another u-turn, shake off Jose, and set up another clear shot, but the change in the breeze brought me back to reality and woke me up from that state of shock. Before they completed their second u-turn, I ran towards a small street, hoping to find the people that I was kicking it with. As I ran down the street, I began to wonder if I made a worse mistake, considering the darkness. As I ran, I began to recreate various scenes in my mind. I envisioned guys shooting at me, someone shooting back, neighbors running out of their home to get the *chisme*, a huge brawl, royal rumble style where everyone was throwing down with everyone. Some of the stories that I was creating in my mind, as I desperately ran for my life, were silly while others were making my heartbeat faster. In the background, I could hear cars cruising on Laurel Canyon filled with the commotion of a festive environment. I wondered if anyone knew or cared about what was happening. As I ran through the darkness of the streets the incident served as a reminder as to why I never really cared for cruising. I was always scared of who I would bump into. I felt the same way about house parties and nightclubs. I ran through a few side streets until I found the guys I was kicking it with. All of them knew the risk of taking me cruising, and immediately sensed the danger. Upon seeing me, they noticed my state of panic. They reacted with the same level of urgency in which I approached them and did not request an explanation. They simply jumped in the car and waited for me to speak. I jumped in the back seat where I was hiding and looking out at the same time. I never saw Jose again. Years later, there I stood before his little sister - a student in my class, and I will never forget what he did for me. What a small world.

I stared at the photograph for a few more seconds before I asked about her relationship with everyone in the picture. She told me they were her siblings and did not believe me when I told her that I knew them: until I pointed them out by name. I found out that Jose was serving time in prison - a twenty-five year to life sentence. He took the wrap for something that his homeboys did. I believed it, even if the jury found him guilty. She was shocked that I knew her siblings. I continued supervising the test and dealt privately with the memories that cluttered my mind, they were not all bad or dangerous. I should have known that teaching at my alma mater would have brought back certain memories.

Although that memory was triggered by looking at a photograph on a students' folder, today I find myself thinking of Jose more than ever before. I now teach at San Fernando High School, the location where I could have lost my life. The site of the shooting that almost was.

Senior Ditch Day

A former student called me to share her enthusiasm about registering for college, but was very disappointed at not placing in English 101, the basic college level English needed to receive a four-year degree. Instead, she placed at a lower level and needed to take additional courses in order to enroll in English 101. During our conversation, she reflected on all of her hard work while taking advance placement (AP) and honors courses. She even excelled at calculus, yet she could not pass an exam to place her at college level English. She asked where I had placed when I first got to college, and without thinking about it, I told her English 21, but thanks to the poor computer systems, was able to jump right into English 28 then 101. I did not think much about what I had said until a few days later. I never took an AP or honors course. I completed high school without ever reading an entire book, yet we tested in the same English class. As a matter of fact, my experience in taking college courses was like taking ESL classes all over again. It was frustrating to not be able to properly articulate my thoughts. A few times my frustration turned to rage and the class discussion became really ugly and tense. In a matter of seconds, I would be ready to throw everything away. I figured I had nothing to lose, for I could not lose what I never had. I would go home angry for not being able to articulate my point. My entire life within the public educational system flashed before me. With rage flowing through my veins, I laughed cynically "the school system is a joke!"

The irony is that the district claims that schools are doing better because the test scores have risen. Yet I was not surprised to hear her story of not being able to place in a college level English class. I have heard this story too many times from other well-disciplined students. This young woman is a fighter. Instead of letting this demoralize her, she took this as a challenge to prove others wrong.

I took basic math two to three years before I was finally able to take Algebra the summer of my junior year; I was not expecting to go to college. Since I did not do well in the summer course, I stopped taking Algebra and never took another math class. Of course I later paid the price for that in college and then again in graduate school. The word calculus was not in my vocabulary. I did not even know how to spell it! I never took trigonometry or geometry, yet I managed to work my way through the university system and successfully get a masters degree in Urban Planning at UCLA. For a while, I saw my accomplishments as the result of my "hustling." Now I understand that it was more than a hustle, it was commitment and hard work.

This incident got me to think about the rest of my students who are not taking AP or honors classes. If she did not place into English 101, what can we expect of the overwhelming majority of students who do not take honors or AP courses?

What is it about our schools that allow students to take college preparatory courses, tell them they are college bound, and not prepare them for the unexpected? Students like me who never read an entire book in high school cannot complain about our starting point in college. I suppose we could ask, and I did ask myself many times, "Why would the district give me a high school diploma if I cannot read at a basic level?" More importantly, what is it that enables some students to excel while others merely squeak by? Is it an inherent drive or their environment? I ponder these questions even more when I travel to other countries. While visiting countries throughout Latin America it is obvious that not everyone goes to school. Yet everywhere I meet young adults and teenagers who impress me with their wealth of knowledge and critical thinking. During my visit in Venezuela, I was having a conversation with a nine-year old boy about their country's President Hugo Chavez. He stated, "Chavez and Bush do not like each other." When he asked where I lived, my reply was, "Los Angeles, California." First, he knew exactly where it was located geographically. Second, he stated, "that use to belong to Mexico." His statement blew me away. I wondered what they are teaching in Venezuela to have a nine-year old boy know these things and why most high school students in the U.S. do not know this basic knowledge.

Our conversation also got me to reflect on the educational content that we are required to teach. This past year I was "written up" for introducing Christopher Columbus, the affects of the conquest, European immigrants, the Mexican American war, and discussing the U.S. invasion of Iraq. I was told that the material "Is not in our State standards." Basically, the U.S. history course teaches students about the American Revolution and with the exception of the French Revolution, all other revolutions are nonexistent. Cuba provides the best and most recent example of a successful revolution. The U.S. history texts ignore this historical event. Too many students are leaving high school thinking that the war in Iraq is solely connected to terrorism and September 11th. The media does not share the stories of the orphanages or civilian casualties of the war. I suppose that may or may not be the media's job, but schools are not teaching students to think critically about anything other than what the media reports. One does not have the option to question. Public speaking and protesting, which are features of our democracy are actually discouraged at schools. A case in point is that many students at SFHS were given a citation for protesting anti-immigration policies and marching in support of immigrant rights on May 1, 2006. Yet the day after the protest, a student returned to class who had been ditching for two weeks and was not cited. Such injustice! What lesson in democracy did this particular student learn? My youngest brother Alex was one of the students cited. I went with him to court, and I spoke with parents of other students who were unjustly cited. The court system also failed to teach students a proper lesson in democracy. The court asked twenty students at a time to stand before a judge. The judge then asked them, "Were you in school during these hours, yes or no?" Every one of them said no and were found guilty. The judge then directed them to the clerk to pay the $200 fine or assign them to a day of community service. The judge refused to hear anything other than yes or no. Hundreds of students were fined that day, and hundreds more on days thereafter. Their lesson in democracy will forever be imprinted in their juvenile record and memory. Most of them will never again participate in a civil or democratic activity, and society will criticize them for their newfound "apathy."

Going back to the question of what the district is teaching students. Democracy is the foundation from which this nation is built on and the expansion of democracy is the latest excuse as to why the United States is in Iraq. Democracy is based on the fundamental right to choose. So let us take a look at two similar choices that many students were confronted with and how the district handled them. First, many students chose not to go to school and protest immigrant rights. The district's action was to cite them. Many anti-immigration teachers purposely gave tests on the day of the protest. Second, students ditched on "Senior Ditch Day," a traditional high school ritual. The district and teachers turned a blind eye and did not penalize students for ditching. Students advise teachers when Senior Ditch Day will occur. They let us know as a courtesy so we will not prepare lessons for that day. I have never heard a student complain that a teacher purposely assigned a test on that day. So what is the district teaching our children? Why are they penalized for acting on a constitutional right while there are no penalties for an unauthorized student-imposed day off from school?

As the day of the well-publicized immigration protest neared, the district spent tax dollars to send letters home encouraging parents to send their children to school on the day of the protest. Yet I have seen no effort made to keep the seniors in school on senior ditch day. Even seniors who are at the risk of not graduating ditch. Yet the district does little to reach out to parents to end Senior Ditch Day. At SFHS security tends to be tighter up until homeroom session. By then the Average Daily Allowance (ADA) is collected and the effort to keep the students on campus is negligible.

Every spring semester when we near Senior Ditch Day, I remember my Senior Ditch Day. We did what most high school students do on senior ditch day; we went to the beach. When we arrived at the beach, a lot of seniors, some juniors, and a few sophomores, including those from other high schools, were already there. With the beach getting overcrowded and having no adult supervision, I began to sense the tension that stemmed from the various rivalries. Whether it was sports related or gangs, the rivalry was real and palpable. Everything was going well and students were setting up, making themselves at home. A few began to jump in the water, while the rest socialized. A small group of guys started throwing the football around and within minutes a small scrimmage of tackle football was under way. The game had just begun when a fight broke out. The natural reaction of young adults is to go see the fight, but there was no time because an entire brawl of ten to twenty guys had begun. Everyone started running away. It turned out that gangs from Pacoima and San Fernando were throwing down. The problem was that you could not tell who was who or whose side they were on. Within seconds, the fight grew and it was no longer just Pacoima and San Fernando. It was everyone who looked like they could be from either gang. Everyone was confused for a gang member including skaters, taggers, nerds, and jocks. It started with "Where are you from?" and continued with "What are you looking at?" Either way, any guy who they wanted to pound on was screwed. At that point, everyone started running towards his or her car as bottles began to fly. Within minutes the helicopters, camera crews, and law enforcement was there. I was hiding from the flying bottles as well as the camera crews. That was the last place I wanted my family to see me. I saw guys run as blood dripped down their faces. My group of friends eventually made it out safe. We were undecided where we would go finish out our ditch day, but we all agreed that we would be staying away from any venue that attracted many high school students.

Aside from Senior Ditch Day, there are other school endorsed days where administrators turn a blind eye when students leave the campus. I wonder what taxpayers, parents, and public officials would say about the school culture the day after finals are over, but actual school time remains. At LAUSD, students still have to attend school after taking their final exam. They expect all students to attend and continue coursework. The expectation is different from the reality. First, it makes no sense that students continue going to class after they have taken their final exam and their grades are submitted. What is there to do? If a student has failed the class, the grade is not going to change. Second, if teachers have submitted grades, (which are due the day following the final) what lessons do we prepare? Students walk around campus begging teachers to let them use the television sets to connect their PlayStation or they look for teachers to let them have a party. My first year teaching I got suckered into allowing the use of my classroom for a party and within minutes the students brought in a boom box, chips, soda, and a lot of their friends. The desks were piled into the corners, the lights were turned off, and students began to dance. The news spread so fast that I had a standing room only party within minutes. One of the assistant principals dropped by to check out the scene and told me "I did not see anything, just don't leave it unsupervised." My colleague from the classroom next door came over to join the fun. She laughed in disbelief. All I could say was, "I agreed with the intention of getting students out of the hallways to avoid bigger problems." After that experience, I have never allowed another end-of-the-year party. At SFHS, the administration does everything possible to keep the students in school the first part of the day in order to collect the Average Daily Allowance. As soon as that happens, the hallways slowly empty out as we get closer to the end of the day. The message to students would change, "If you are not going to attend class, then go home but you can not be walking around the hallway." The gates are left open and unattended, making it easier for students to leave campus. Of course, if they went to their assigned class they would find their teachers working on grades or cleaning out the cupboards. Technically, by then we had "covered all of the standards" and since we are instructed to teach the standards only, we are done with the curriculum as soon as the final exams are given.

This past year a former student who should have graduated the previous year, was notified during graduation rehearsal that he would not be participating in the ceremony. According to the administrators, the student had exceeded the minimum number of absences permitted to graduate on stage. I suppose it is only fair that administrators comply with school policy.

Walkout 2006

Today marks a new day for the high school. For the first time in my four years of teaching at San Fernando High School the students took a collaborative stance and walked out in the most respectful and orderly fashion. As far as I know, little to no onsite planning took place for this event, yet hundreds of them took it to the streets in support of a common cause - immigration. It turns out that much of the planning took place on the popular website MySpace. This fascinated me. As I understand, the U.S. government invented the internet as a tool to infiltrate and sabotage the Civil Rights Movement during the 1960s. Now forty or so years later, the youth of the information age have figured out how to use it to their advantage and organize this massive walkout. According to the newspapers, this walkout for immigrant rights was bigger than the East Los Angeles High School Blowouts of the 1960s.

For many years, I have engaged in various discussions with colleagues, classmates, and students on the rebellious apathy of this generation. Unlike the rebellious attitude of the youth from the 1960s who actively opposed the Vietnam War, dealt with segregation in schools and lunch counters, voters rights, gender discrimination and many other social injustices, today's youth are absorbed by digital technology and do not get involved. At the end of every discussion the same question would arise, "What will it take to wake up today's youth?" What will it take for today's youth to drop their video games and pay attention to world events? The war in Iraq stirred some emotion and raised an eyebrow, but not enough for students to take it to the streets in large numbers. But it was a different day on Monday, March 27,

2006. As the students walked out of the school through the main gate, I was overwhelmed with emotion and was speechless. As I attempted to speak, I could feel the lump in my throat. I quietly walked to my classroom as students continued to walk out. Many students waved at me as they marched on the sidewalk and passed by the side gate. I waved back with a lot of pride and respect for those who took a stand. The hair on my arms stood straight. I noticed a student from my fifth period class use her friend to hide from me. If she only knew how proud I was of her. I walked up to my class and went straight to the window. I opened the window to hear the students chant, "SI SE PUEDE, SI SE PUEDE!" The chant made famous by Cesar Chavez and the farm workers' movement. The chanting was harmony to my soul. It was rejuvenating and uplifting to hear their voices echo into the building. A few students looked toward me and waved. The lump in my throat kept me from saying anything. As a sign of support, I waved my fist in the air, but I was too paralyzed with emotion to say anything. I paced back and forth, not knowing what to say or do. I thought of walking out with the students, but immediately realized it would jeopardize my job. As it was, the principal continuously gave me a hard time about the supplemental material that I incorporated into the classroom. I continued to peek through the window and was very surprised to see so many students, who I would never imagine to walk out, stay with the group and march down the sidewalk. As students continued to march on the sidewalk, I could hear the sound of other students in the hallway encouraging each other to leave. Four students arrived to class, and all asked me for permission to leave. I explained to them that I could not give them permission. All four got up and walked out.

I walked to the door, looked out the hallway, and saw other teachers stand in shock. They also seemed to be suppressing their pride and excitement for the protestors. None of the teachers expressed a complaint. Instead, you would hear rumblings like "could you believe..." or "I am surprised that students ..." or "I can't believe that not all of them left." Because we worked for the district, it was not acceptable to openly express any support for students, which meant that I could only have this discussion with the few teachers that I considered allies.

The famous sleeping giant was no longer sleeping. It began to walk. The thought of the giant awakening was scary for those who never imagined it to be possible and exciting for those of us who have been waiting for this day. The heart of the sleeping giant began to beat a lot harder early that morning and the beating only got stronger by the hour. It was a heartbeat that brought life to many of the city's long time passive residents.

In actuality, the students deserved an A for the day for participation. The protest was a sign that students have connected the real world to the instructional material. For many years students learned about great historical figures, such as George Washington who successfully led the colonists to victory in the American Revolution. They learned about the Harriet Tubman who rebelled against slavery (ironically, a system created by the same heroes of the American Revolution). And they learned about the Civil Rights Movement, Martin Luther King Jr. and Rosa Parks. In more recent years, they are now learning about Cesar Chavez and Dolores Huerta, and their contributions to the farm workers' rights and labor movement. I previously wondered if students ever paid attention and cared how these historical leaders impacted their life. This walkout showed me that the students did appreciate these legends. They decided to contribute and create their own historical moment.

This past decade, especially during the Bush administration, there has been a major emphasis on the curriculum standards and standardized testing, known as the California State Test (CST). When I was in high school, the results did not count towards high school graduation and few students took the tests seriously. I was NOT one of them. In order to finish fast and save myself the headache of having to decide what to bubble on the scantron, I would bubble A,B,C,D, then D,C,B,A then return to A,B,C,D, and continue with that pattern throughout the test.

In recent years, most schools show a pattern of improvement in their individual scores. So what! I for one was not impressed with the improved test scores. What did they really mean? Were students marching into class in a single file line reading everything that was being assigned, free of disruption? Were students no longer ditching and spending endless hours in the library studying for their next test?

The walkout and protest against the HR4437 immigration bill was an indicator that students are learning. They definitely understand their first amendment right, as well as the seriousness of HR4437. They may not know all of the details of HR4437, but their general understanding of it was more than enough. As a matter of fact, most teachers had never heard of the bill until the protest. Due to the excessive focus on standards, teachers are highly encouraged to teach to the test, at least at San Fernando High School that is the case. To teach anything that the students will not be tested on is considered a waste of time.

As a teacher, my job is neither to encourage nor discourage their actions. How can I mention the legacy of Cesar Chavez or Martin Luther King Jr., and then discourage students from following their footsteps? More often than not we use these historical figures to inspire the youth of what's possible. If the adults, schools, districts, and or politicians disagree with the action taken by the students I suppose we should ask, "What is the purpose of inspiring youth?" The story of Harriet Tubman is inspirational and it was her defiance towards status quo that guaranteed her a place in history. I doubt that today's society would question her contribution to U.S. history. Equally as valuable is the movement for immigrant rights, as it has become the unifying struggle with Latino students across the nation.

The day following the protest students shared their experience in class. The one theme they shared is that students from rival schools marched together, shared water bottles, and even discussed school sports. How could it be possible that a student from Sylmar High School have a civil conversation with a student from San Fernando High School? These two schools have been rivals for decades. All sporting events between these two schools require extra security. Yet both groups of students, with little to no adult supervision, marched together under a single banner – the stand for basic human rights!

The Joke is on You:
World Cup 2006 vs. Iraq

As I walked to school thinking of the first period lecture, I noticed that more students than usual were walking in the opposite direction. It was not Senior Ditch Day, which had taken place a few weeks earlier. It was not that students were on their way to a protest because the protests and rallies for immigrant rights had already occurred. The majority of these students were wearing Mexico's soccer jersey. I noticed that others had their jersey over their shoulder or a flag hanging out of their back pocket. A few made eye contact, but most did everything possible to avoid looking at me for fear that I would redirect them back to school. None of the students were in my class, nor did I know anyone of them personally. I simply knew they were students at the high school and they were well aware that I was a teacher. I said nothing because I did not have the time or energy to round them up. It was 7:30 AM and redirecting large groups of students back to school was not how I wanted to start my day. As I passed them, I questioned my commitment to them for not saying anything, but quickly justified my silence with thoughts of our poor security and lax administration and the fact that they would leave campus anyway. I was slowly learning that without administrative support, I would soon go crazy rounding up students who chose not to go to class. In the past, veteran teachers advised me to let them go. They had given up years earlier and had stopped checking for hall passes. I have to admit that it is demoralizing to notice that administrators seldom question students roaming the hallways or leaving campus early in the morning. They must think their title and responsibilities are too important to stop students in the hallway. Actually, the high volume of students walking off campus at a time when administrators are standing guard at all gates is clear evidence of their lax attitude. I once complained to Mr. Salsipuedes, one of the six assistant principals, about students walking around during class time making noise and disturbing instruction. His response was "close your door and don't worry about what goes on outside!" I complained to Principal Mr. Salinas, but his shock seemed to be from the transparency of Mr. Salsipuedes and not from the herds of students who freely walk around campus. Needless to say, the principal did nothing.

Seeing students walk in the opposite direction reminded me of my days in high school when I thought I knew everything. Few adults could reason with me because I thought that I understood everything that makes the world turn. At least that was my front. The reality was different; I was insecure and did not have a clue as to the direction of my life. I knew what I did not want, but I didn't know what I did want. I knew that I did not want to work as hard as my father. I knew that I did not want to work as much as my mother who oftentimes cleaned houses on the weekend in order to provide a few extra dollars for the family. Both of my parents worked full-time and still had a side hustle selling clothes, recycling cans, cleaning houses, selling tamales on Saturday's, or any other job that would make a few extra bucks. As the oldest child, I was always by their side contributing. I knew then that I did not want to live this way forever, but did not know the specifics of what I wanted. I worked by their side until I was able to work independent of them, but continued to help them when my schedule permitted.

Not knowing what I wanted in life gave me little incentive to take school seriously. Even though I thought school was a joke, it felt like we were being taught the same thing every year. I ditched as often as possible and rarely spent an entire day in school. The only class where I consistently attended was Period 6, football. In all of my other classes I worked hard enough to get by. An "A" was just as good as a "C." They both gave me the credits that I needed to pass the class. Here I was, sixteen years later working with students and seeing students who were a carbon copy of me when I was in school, thinking that they understand how their choices affect their present and future.

That afternoon Mexico played Angola in the World Cup and students were on their way to see it live. If they only knew that they did not have to ditch school to see the game. It turned out that in the second floor of the 500 building every other classroom was showing it. Students anxiously walked around with antennas looking for the classroom with the best reception. The game began during period four, which was my conference period. I was adjusting the monitor for reception when a couple of students walked in and asked if they could join me. I agreed to allow them only if they presented me with a permission slip from their period four teacher. I figured that would be enough of a prerequisite to avoid having them yell in my room every time Mexico scored a goal. They returned within minutes accompanied by other friends, and all had a note from their teachers. By then it was noticeable that other classrooms were also setting their curriculum aside to watch the game.

As the minutes passed and Mexico struggled to dominate Angola, I could not believe the energy and fervor that filled the building. I could hear students in other rooms take a deep sigh or mumble with desperation as team Angola was slipping right through the fingertips of Mexico. I laughed in disbelief when I realized what had become of the school; I doubt that the second floor of the 500 building was the only place where the game was being watched. Fifteen minutes into the game, a couple of students arrived with sodas and chips. Not surprisingly, they snuck out to go to the store and managed to sneak back in carrying huge plastic bags that contained sodas and chips. Leaving campus was no big deal. One of the students felt so comfortable about the World Cup environment at SFHS that he hung the Mexican flag outside of my window, which was on the second floor and faced the street. I took it down as soon as I saw it. I did not want to advertise the game in my room nor did I want to trigger a discussion with anti-immigrant teachers at the school.

Internally I continued to laugh. I laughed at the fact that students were running the show at SFHS. They were calling the shots that period. They requested to see the World Cup and their request was granted. I laughed in disbelief at the fact that administration was nowhere in sight, although that was nothing new. I laughed at the fact that I was not afraid if administration visited my class. I continued to laugh in frustration when I realized that I was more afraid to discuss the war in Iraq. Administration had placed several memos in my file for not following state standards and for discussing Iraq. But that was not good enough for Principal Mr. Salinas; they continued placing memos in my file for anything and everything. I was instructed to stick to the State standards, but the standards at SFHS were so low that I was having a difficult time following instructions. I sat back and laughed with thoughts of the principal sitting is his office watching Mexico struggle to dominate Angola.

As I sat and amused myself with thoughts of the Principal Salinas watching the game and placing wagers, I could not stop observing how attentive the students were. One bad pass by Mexico and they dragged their behinds to the edge of the seat; some pulled their hair while others covered their eyes and threw their heads back. "Wow, if only they could be this engaged in class," I said to myself. I thought of the many students who left school early that morning to see the game. "If they only knew that the joke was on them," I continued thinking to myself. Some students walked all over the school district thinking that they were in charge. If they only knew that, the joke was on them. I wondered how many of the students watching the World Cup are reading at grade level.

I began to think of my own brother Alex, a fourteen-year-old freshman in high school who also likes to think that he knows everything. He once told me, "You did it. Why not let others experience things for themselves?" I questioned if he ever pays attention to the conversations of other adults where they tirelessly complain of not having taken advantage of their opportunities provided to them when they were young.

There I was with a large group of students who were fully engaged on the game, despite having drama at home, school, and everywhere else in their life. I enjoyed watching their enthusiasm for the game, one that I rarely saw in class. Granted one cannot compare economics or history to a World Cup game, but the enthusiasm that I wished to see in class was not for the textbook knowledge that came out of economics or history, rather the enthusiasm to go into the world, take on their life and apply everything that they are learning. I immediately shifted my thoughts and began to think of the many lessons they were learning at such young age.

I thought of the many athletes who are taken advantage of by both their parents and coaches. As soon as their athletic talent is discovered, everyone begins to think "pros," college ball, and endorsements. Thoughts of the fathers and coaches who want teenagers to succeed in sports more so than the athletes themselves. In my years of teaching and coaching various little leagues, I have concluded that most of the absolutely best players never get to play their professional sport. The overwhelming majority do not have grades and another handful develop a horrible attitude. Yet too many coaches and parents alike focus so much on sports that they completely ignore academics. I once had a star soccer player enroll two weeks late into class. He was in South America at a youth tournament. He never turned in his homework and began to arrive late to class. When I called the mother to discuss my concern, she immediately attempted to explain that her son and I both had strong personalities and it would be best if he was placed in another class. I later found out that she was a single mother and her son never had a male figure challenge him. At the mother's request, the son was transferred to another class. I would later see him roaming the halls acting up and skipping class. He was failing a couple of classes, so his mentality became, "Why bother going to any class." I have never understood this phenomenon. Failing a class with LAUSD is a difficult thing to do. Students almost have to go out of their way to fail a class. Although I was a knucklehead and ditched a lot throughout my high school years, I never failed a class.

On another occasion, a football player was failing my class, which would make him ineligible to play after the midterm progress report card. The mother came to me and requested that I change the grade so her son could play against Sylmar High School. Sylmar is San Fernando's biggest school rival. She also wanted him to be eligible for wrestling, which would begin when football season ended. The wrestling coach also asked me to change the grade. I told them both that I would think about it, and struggled with my decision for a couple of days. I had never changed a grade before. On the morning of the deadline I told the coach that I would not be changing the grade, he casually replied "That's fine, don't worry about it." That same Friday, San Fernando and Sylmar High School squared off on the football field. I went out to see the game and the failing student was the first person I noticed on the field. He was waving his helmet during the break off from a team huddle. I could not believe my eyes and felt cheated by the coach, the student, the school, the parents, the district, and anyone who knew that the student was ineligible. I later found out that coach got another teacher to raise his grade, which automatically raised his GPA. I was also shocked to discover that athletes are eligible to play even with two "Fs," as long as he or she has a 2.0 GPA. What a joke! No wonder few if any of our student athletes ever go to a four-year university, especially football players. This adds to a bigger issue, one of low expectations. Actually, it is a bit worse, one of NO expectations! Students are not even expected to pass their core classes in order to play sports. When I was in school, sports were used as the carrot to pass all of the classes and maintaining a minimum GPA of 2.0. Actually, this policy may be older than me, and it is possible that I was under the impression that I needed to pass all of my classes. With this minimum 2.0 GPA eligibility requirement, a student athlete could maintain an "A" in sports, an "A" in their elective, an "F" in two core classes, and a "C" in two other classes. Our sports program was more valuable than academic achievement. The year before we had a wrestling star who won the city championship and placed third in the state. He was also a star running back. However, the focus on sports over education took him straight to a community college. There is nothing wrong with a community college, as that was my career starting point. The student retention rate is what concerns me. Fifty percent of all community college students do not return their second year, much less go on to a four-year university.

We should not be surprised to find out that UCLA enrolled only ninety-six Black students in the fall of 2006. Of those ninety-six Black students, twenty are recruited athletes. Critics of UCLA's admissions practice have placed the entire blame on UCLA, but how about sharing that blame with their feeder schools and districts who continue lowering their academic expectations for students in general. It is known that Black males are heavily recruited into high school football and basketball teams. It is also known that if the schools were not using them for sports, many of them would be ignored or pushed aside. I have heard school personnel say, "Sports are the only thing that keeps them in school." I question if it is the other way around, "Sports is the reason schools don't completely push them aside." When I arrived to college, I made the football team as a kicker. I quit during spring training and later returned during the summer. Again, I was able to make the team and got a small taste of being a college athlete. Back then, one had to stand in three-hour lines to register for classes and purchase books. I never had to do either one. My football jersey gave me the privilege to walk to the front of the line. It was also obvious that if I ever broke my leg I would have to stand with everyone else. That privilege ended quickly when I purposely missed the bus to our first game and decided that I was through entertaining others. It was too obvious that the coaches were only looking out for their best interest in building a good team and suggested that I take courses that were easy to pass. None of their suggested courses counted towards my major. I already felt illiterate enough; I did not need their help to make matters worse.

After the wrestling coach got another teacher to change my student's grade, I filed a complaint with administration. Ms. Simple, one of the assistant principals (who has been promoted to Principal since then) told me to not take it personal and get accustomed to coaches asking me to change grades, "Although I don't encourage it, it is part of the high school culture," she admitted. Ms. Simple added, "Many people take high school sports very seriously." That was not the answer I was expecting to hear. Therefore, I suggested that it was more than high school sports. It was an overall culture of low expectations. I explained to her how the previous week only four students had turned in their homework. She placed all responsibility on me and suggested that I may not have given proper instructions. "It was a current event," I replied, "an assignment that all students are familiar with at an early age." She asked if I had provided students with the newspaper. No, I replied. I should not have to give students a newspaper. Ms. Simple then proceeded to explain, "The students we serve at this school are very special. Many of them live three or four families to a house. Some even live an entire family to a bedroom and money is a big factor." "Fifty cents to a dollar is all a newspaper costs," I replied with frustration. "Have you not noticed the expensive shoes that most students are wearing, and the bags of Hot Cheetos they purchase everyday in the student store?" Ms. Simple, not wanting to be challenged began to walk away and stated, "Then you deal with the problem, since you seem to have it all figured out."

Ms. Simple's perception is that students are so poor that everything must be provided, even a newspaper. Where do we draw the line? Should we not expect students and their families to invest fifty cents worth in education?

In the case of the student athlete, he was caught a couple of weeks later selling weed on campus. He was kicked out of school. The idea that sports would save him from falling into temptation is only partially true. I am not disputing that high school sports do not support young male students from ending up in gangs or drugs, but that is only a temporary solution. The current sports culture does not help engage students in academic achievement.

Sports alone will not save any student. I once saw a documentary on Sports Center about professional athletes who still have ties to gangs. This attitude of sports being an alternative to gangs is one of pity that allows student athletes to only be athletes. In four years, I have seen a lot of athletic talent. None of these student athletes has made it to a major university. Athletes have told me that coaches discourage them from taking my class and enrolling into a class with a teacher who will guarantee a passing grade needed for eligibility. My brother, who is in the magnet program, was encouraged to leave the magnet program and take regular classes. That way, he could avoid taking rigorous classes and make it easier to be eligible for sports. The magnet program has a graduation rate of ninety eight percent, whereas the regular school has a graduation rate of less than fifty percent. This sort of bad advice should be considered a criminal activity or a hate crime. The effects of this type of advice cannot be measured.

A culture of low expectations is one that is teaching students to live in scarcity rather than abundance and settling for the bare minimum. The bare minimum is a piece of paper that we call a high school diploma. A student who does not see the value of spending fifty cents on a newspaper to complete their homework is being prepared to not see value in investing in himself or herself. Students who are not able to earn their spot on any sports team, because of their low GPA, will struggle with issues of self worth.

On a separate occasion, I was encouraged by Ms. Acrimony to make an exception to my class rules and give Pepe, one of my students, an opportunity to make up the necessary work to pass the class and graduate. Pepe was a super senior (fifth year in high school) who had twenty-five class absences and over thirty missing assignments. He was a super senior who drove a Mercedes Benz to school, but could not attend outside activities that provided extra credit because he had to work to make the car payments. During a parent-teacher conference, Pepe's mother and Ms. Acrimony "encouraged" me to give him a second chance. Ms. Acrimony stated, "Let's work with him. He really seems to want to graduate this year." I am not sure how she arrived to that conclusion. Again, what is the lesson that Pepe is being taught by his mother and assistant principal? She simply wants her son to have a diploma and it does not matter how he obtains it. The assistant principal wants to please the mother, at the expense of Pepe's future. Although both adults are acting with the best of intentions, the effects of their "altruism" on Pepe's life are negative and immeasurable. He will spend the rest of his life knowing that he did not legitimately earn his diploma.

I could share more stories. The bottom line is that we have reached a point in time when even parents, not knowing any better, contribute to "academic" social promotion. What lesson is learned by the above-mentioned students or others with similar stories? Although students cannot immediately realize the negative effects of "getting by" in school, they eventually pay a great price for being part of a system that promoted them without any expectation. To many teenagers it may seem funny to graduate from high school without ever having read an entire book, as I did. It is not funny when, as an adult, you are buying a car or a house and the financing and paperwork confuses you. It is not funny when you do not know how to complete a job application or write a résumé. Most high school graduates do not possess the most basic skills needed to fill out their own financial aid application for college. I was one of the students who "just got by" through high school. Although I had made it, I realized that I had not hustled the district for my diploma, rather the district hustled me out of an education.

Math 81

"Three days left of school," I announced to the class as I changed the number of days left of school, written on the board. It seemed like yesterday when I began the 50-day countdown. Initially many students dismissed the countdown, despite feeling a bit of pressure for not having any plans for the future. As days passed, the students' anxiety grew as their unknown future neared. Some even requested that I stop counting.

Along with the countdown, I would periodically ask that they share their plans after high school. Only a handful spoke up and shared. The majority did not have a clue as to what their plans were. This increased their anxiety, which I was aware of, but it was important to me that they think about their future. This class was no different from past graduating seniors. Few students were accepted into four-year universities. Of those students, there were many who would not go onto the university due to their parent's fear of the unknown. The rest of them had no concrete plans and enrolled at a community college. Sadly, many traditional parents were against their son or daughter going away for college, even when expenses were covered. I mainly encountered this dilemma with female students; maybe the male students were ashamed to admit that their parents controlled their life. Either way, female students were the ones to speak up on this issue. On a number of occasions, students invited me to speak to their parents. Unfortunately, most girls would give in to their parents desires instead of their own. Oftentimes, in exchange for not going on to college, parents would bribe their daughter with new cars or other empty promises.

Towards the final weeks of school, the student's anxiety levels increased even more. Anticipation filled their facial expressions. Their smiles expressed a sense of accomplishment. They were smiles that one breaks just before the onset of joyful tears. For many students, they would be the first in their family to cross the graduation stage.

On this particular day when I announced that there were three days left, I felt a mix of emotions and energy levels. One student in particular stood out; she wishes to be referred to as M&M. The expression on her face was one of sadness with tears forming in her eyes. As soon as students started their textbook standards-based work, I called her over. "What is wrong?" I asked. She could not lie. M&M attempted to hold back the tears as she struggled to say, "I can't talk about it or I will cry." I replied with the obvious, "You are already crying." This broke the tension and she started to laugh nervously. But very quickly she became sad. "Please stop mister or you will make me cry more," she replied as she was quickly reminded of the reasons for her tears. "You are already crying," I replied again. Again, she began to laugh as she attempted to hold back her tears. She opted to step outside to talk about her problem.

Once outside I asked again, "So what is the problem?" She knew, like all other students, that she could not lie to me for I knew them too well. I also would not settle for an "I'm just sad" response. I initially expected to hear another "my boyfriend left me" story. Or "my best friend is not talking to me." It was neither. M&M was crying because she had just received her Math and English placement results from the community college. "I placed in Math 81," she stated with so much emotion. "At what level were you expecting to place?" I asked. "I don't know, just not this low." "How am I supposed to test at college level if

I learned nothing in my math classes here?" she offered. According to M&M, by placing at Math 81 she will have to take four to five math classes before completing the college requirements for a bachelor degree.

"What is the highest level of math that you completed?" I asked, "Well I took a year with Ms. Margarita and another with Mr. Paredes," she said disappointingly. If she was mute and I based our conversation on her expressions I would have guessed that she had been kicked out of her house or possibly turned up pregnant. Instead, she was mentioning the names of two teachers who have a horrible reputation on campus. Unfortunately for M&M, she had both teachers for math. Ms. Margarita was late to class at least two to three times per week and frequently absent. According to students, she would buy them donuts for behaving well and fully participating whenever an administrator was present. Ms. Margarita was absent so frequently that I covered her classes quite often. Ms. Margarita's class always reminded me of a Hollywood blockbuster movie where unruly youth run the class. The desks were tagged with graffiti as if no adult was ever there to supervise. Essentially, Ms. Margarita was known to pass students based on behavior, not on academics. Over the years it was well known that Ms. Margarita sat through the entire class eating while her top students taught the class.

Mr. Paredes was slightly different. He never missed class. He was so committed to working that he taught during all of his vacations. Mr. Paredes had a reputation of not knowing math. According to students, he was frequently corrected by the top students in the class. During nutrition and lunch, I recall the man only talk about sex and nothing worth sharing outside of the teacher's cafeteria. That was my experience of these two math teachers and poor M&M had them both. Unfortunately, the teacher's union was too strong and a complaint would not do any good. At worst, both would be transferred to another school.

M&M began to share her experience. "Come on Gutierrez, you know about Ms. Margarita, she never teaches anything. I was able to pass her class just by treating her nicely." I asked about Mr. Paredes. "How did you pass his class?" "Well with him nobody was passing the class except for a couple of students. One of them always wore mini skirts and Mr. Paredes would stare at her legs the entire period. He even sat her in the front so he could look at her the entire period. She never took a test and yet always had a passing score. When I noticed this I also began to wear mini skirts and low tops." M&M blushed a bit. It was clear she was not proud of herself and did whatever worked for her. Students would complain but little was done, which meant that students were stuck in math classes with teachers they could not respect. Ms. Margarita and Mr. Paredes were teachers who would not be trusted with the children of their own colleagues.

M&M then asked, "How else was I supposed to pass? Nobody passes his class. Everyone fails his tests because he cannot teach. He would get mad when students asked him questions because he didn't know the answer." I shook my head in disbelief. "How could a teacher get mad at students for asking a question?" I silently asked myself. I continued to shake my head in disbelief. The horror stories of these teachers were well known and administration did nothing about it. No one had to say anything. The stories were out in the open yet silenced by adults who did not have the courage to take action. Whenever students attempted to change classes, to avoid more work, counselors and administrators would often tell students,

"Now with Standards, all teachers are teaching the same material." M&M continued with her story. "I would wear low tops and show my cleavage on the day of the test, then walk up to his desk and press my arms together when I asked him a question. He would tell me not to worry about it and I was able to pass the tests and eventually the class."

"Well there you go," I said, "now you get to take Math 81!" The tears stopped as she burst into laughter. I shared a bit about my experience with math and the struggles I endured even through graduate school.

I pointed out how much she had contributed to her low placement in math and English. She acknowledged her responsibility, but was still frustrated, disappointed, and hurt. She felt betrayed by the school system and herself.

In general, the students and parents at the school were complacent. This had a lot to do with the poor reception by administration. In previous meetings, many parents expressed frustration with the school, but had bought into the idea that makes so many immigrant families feel guilty about complaining or setting demands, "It is better than where you came from," and "be happy you were able to make it this far."

She admitted to have never shared this story with anyone prior to our conversation. She was definitely ashamed and would now pay the consequences at the college level. She was not alone. I inquired about English. She took an AP English class her senior year yet tested at English 21, two classes below the required level for a bachelor degree. "How could that be possible, she asked?" For this exact same reason, I reminded M&M; an "A" at San Fernando HS does not carry the same weight, or is comparable to an "A" from Beverly Hills High School. I remembered reading an article published in the Daily News that stated, "D students from Beverly Hills High School attend college at the same rate as "A" students from Sylmar High School." Sylmar and San Fernando High Schools have similar student body populations.

I half-jokingly told her that I would one day write an essay titled Math 81. She was torn between laughing at herself and laughing out of nervousness. But M&M immediately gave me the okay. "More people need to know about what goes on at SFHS" were her final words. We returned to class as she wiped the tears of her face. I reminded M&M that I would title it Math 81 and she burst into laughter.

Some students were confused about her laughter with clear evidence of tears and sadness behind her giggles. No one said a word and continued working. Some students were simply reminded of the love-hate relationship they have with SFHS. This was the place were they spent some memorable years. For some students, SFHS is where they first fell in love or experienced their first kiss. For many, this would be the final destination of being an innocent child. Yet this place with so many great memories ill prepared them for the challenges that await them in the adult world. One thing in their favor is that these students are survivors. They knew how to figure things out and manage adversity. Some had spent a couple of weeks crossing the desert in order to study at SFHS. A good number of them lived with their relatives instead of their parents for their parents are undocumented and lived in Mexico. It was common for these students to express their frustration for the abuse they endured by their guardian and their sadness for the long distance between them and their parents. Regardless of their situation, they all learned to survive in a school that was overcrowded and that expected little of them. All of the new arrivals would finish four years of ESL (English as a Second Language) and four years of English concurrently. It was incredible how dedicated they were, attending adult school, intersession, Saturday school, and any other school that would advance them with their English. Surviving was the name of the game.

To all current and future high school students: I wish that by writing this essay I could eliminate all of the individual and institutional injustices found in schools. The reality is ugly. There is a shortage of teachers accompanied by the high turnover rate. The teacher's union puts the schools in a peculiar situation; one that does not place student needs and safety at the top of the list. For the many students that graduated, they survived an obstacle course that was not always defined. This obstacle course changed from one day to the next. Congratulations if you were flexible and figured it out. For the students who did not graduate, grades are only part of your education. You have received another type of education. Now go back and get the grades.

Where They End Up, I Don't Always Know

It never fails that a small group of students from every graduating class will stay in contact throughout their college experience and eventually invite me to their graduation. For some of them, I become a college advisor as they sometimes struggle through their college major selection process. I have had many students express an interest within the different levels of education. It is always flattering to hear them wanting to teach the social sciences.

With some students, I have become good friends with their entire family. One family that comes to mind lives a few blocks away from my home. The level of trust is so strong that during one of my trips, Myrna, who is a former student, picked up my mail. Going into the profession I never expected to become good friends with students. I knew that I would have good relationships while they were in class, but never a long lasting relationship with the entire family. Myrna has successfully completed her BA and is now a social worker. She intends to get her teaching credential and eventually pursue a career with the district.

Our relationship has been great, one where we will occasionally get together for a drink or even go to a protest. For many years Myrna dated the same guy from high school, so he has always known of our friendship. I mention her ex-boyfriend because on occasion with other female students a jealous boyfriend or husband made it impossible for some students to stay in touch.

Over the years, my students have inspired me. Some for their academic achievement and others for their will to overcome any obstacle that gets in the way. During my first year of teaching, I met a young lady named Fabiola whose mother died of cancer shortly after we met. I expected her to lose interest in school. A couple of us teachers who knew of her mother's death were waiting for the day that she gave up, not because she was a slacker, but because of the unexpected tragedy she was facing. As the oldest in her family, like most traditional families, Fabiola played a major role at home. Her father was an alcoholic and struggled to hold a steady job. Overnight Fabiola became a mom to her younger brother and fought hard to stay on top of her studies. At times, she reminded me of my own mother who also lost her mother at sixteen to cancer. Both were fighters and were too stubborn to take no for an answer. When Fabiola realized that she was not on an academic track, she demanded a switch of classes and enrolled in all college prep courses. Initially, after her mother's death, she was determined to go to medical school and work with cancer patients. She was accepted at a private college where she obtained a BA in Political Science. Although she has yet to pursue her original interest, Fabiola has served as a great source of personal inspiration. Being witness to her determination to overcome all odds, Fabiola also kept me to my word about continuing with graduate school and constantly reminded me of my passion and career goals. Fabiola is now living with the father of her little girl.

Not all of my encounters with former students have been pleasant. This past baseball season I bumped into a former student at Dodger Stadium. Unfortunately, my past got in the way of us being able to cordially greet each other. He was one of the first students that I had while teaching in my alma mater. He was one of a handful of students who held me to my past. When he found out that I was a former gang member from his rival neighborhood, he checked out of class and stopped talking to me. I'm not sure if he was a younger brother or relative to one of the guys that I boxed it out with or if he was just too prideful to leave my past behind. Either way, his silent treatment in the classroom and hallways served as a constant reminder of my past. At times, the silent treatment triggered a sense of guilt. While at other times, I too would get a bit prideful and dismiss it with a big "Fuck it!" attitude. It was obvious that I was no longer the same person and that my students came first. It was his choice to hold onto the past. I was again reminded of my past when I encountered him at the Dodger Stadium ten years later. At the end of the day, I knew that my conscience was clean and was able to enjoy the game without paying attention to his resentment and negative energy.

Last year I bumped into a group of former students who gave me an update on several of their classmates. The update of everyone was overshadowed by the story of Silvio. I still remember when Silvio first came to my class. His mother escorted him to his first class ever in the United States. When I opened the door and welcomed him in – his mother stated, "se lo encargo maestro," *I leave him in your hands*. I promised to look after Silvio and provide him with the necessary guidance to acclimate at that enormous school with approximately 4,200 students. For those of us who grew up here, the craziness of a year-round school was normal. However, for Silvio, someone who was coming from a remote village in Mexico, the student population far exceeded the total population of his village. This was the experience of many students from Central America and Mexico.

Silvio was quiet and dressed in humble clothes. Although his hair was long enough to cover his forehead, it was obvious that someone in the family had cut it. I could identify with his home-style hair cut from personal experience as I also had haircuts at home. In many ways, Silvio reminded me of when I first started elementary school. We were so poor that my mother was also the family hairstylist. My dad tried it once, but clipped a piece of my ear. That was enough for my mother to ban him from cutting anyone's hair. After realizing that he clipped a piece of my ear, he smirked with amusement and embarrassment. I can still remember taking a shower and feeling a sharp sting on the wound.

Silvio came and went to class without a single word leaving his mouth. This was his pattern for a while. I could tell that other students, who had been in the states for a longer period, would indirectly point out to each other Silvio's humble clothes. Silvio was timid and shy but not stupid. He knew exactly who they were talking about. But he said nothing. With time, Silvio was accepted by the same group that initially gave him a difficult time. They had all experienced it and simply felt the need to try it on the new student.

Over time, Silvio slowly began to acculturate himself to his new home. His clothes slowly got baggier and trendier. Within a year's time, Silvio shaved his head and walked in excessively baggy clothes. He continued to be timid in class, but his classmates would constantly put him on the spot and heckle him in my presence. He simply stayed quiet and desperately waited for the attention to shift towards a different classmate.

Before long I could not recognize the humble Silvio I once knew. He was fully acculturated. Even the Black students, who tended to tease and harass ESL students, left Silvio alone. His presence commanded respect or should I say his baggy clothes, shaved head, strut, and body language commanded the respect. I suppose it did not matter to Silvio that his appearance was commanding respect, he was simply relieved to be left alone. Every now and then, he would stop by and generate small talk with me. I could tell he felt uncomfortable in his excessively baggy clothes. It seemed like Silvio was relieved to be himself in my presence and would drop his guard. In some ways, I could not blame him. The Black, as well as the second and third generation Mexican students tended to be extremely brutal with the ESL students who were primarily from El Salvador, Guatemala, Mexico, Nicaragua, and Honduras. Some of the hecklers were immigrants themselves who came at an early age and had experienced the brutal treatment but now needed to pass it on.

Silvio's experience constantly reminded me of my own experience. One of the first personal incidents in which race played a critical role for me was when I was jumped by two Black students in the third grade. The worst part about having to fight two Black students was seeing White teachers stand around and do nothing about it. In desperation, I cried for help. By the end of the fight, I remember being mad at the White teachers for not intervening. I was not angry at the Black students for jumping me. Now, as a teacher I would not dare stand on the sideline and let other students do the same.

These encounters also reminded me of my days in middle school. ESL students would always come to my homeboys and me for protection - primarily from Black students and the occasional White students. A few times this led to major brawls between the Blacks and us. There I was, fifteen or so years later, seeing the same incident unfold before my eyes.

Nevertheless, Silvio no longer had to worry. He was safe underneath his new identity. Silvio was fully integrated into the urban American way of life. He was as American as apple pie. He joined a gang and he was no longer one of "them," a *chunt, chunty, wetback, paisa* (derogatory terms used to disrespect Latinos). Silvio was now a homeboy. He was never open with me about his involvement. I found out through his friends who every now and then would heckle him in my presence. I also began to identify the signs through his homemade tattoos, belt buckle, baseball cap, and other paraphernalia that identified him with his new street-adopted family. I am not sure if he was embarrassed to share his affiliation with me. He knew that I was once a member of his now rival gang. However, he also knew that my students came first and that I no longer had any affiliations. Either way Silvio never addressed the issue.

Years later, upon encountering Silvio's classmates they briefed me on his whereabouts. Apparently, Silvio was at the park across the street from his home when a group of guys jumped out of a car and began running after him. Before he could react, Silvio was shot in the chest. He managed to run in desperation, and applied pressure to his chest. Silvio took his last breathe of air in front of his doorstep. I can only suppose he simply wanted to apologize and say good-bye to his mother.

I continue to live with the memory of Silvio's mother at the doorway of my classroom begging that I look out for her son, "Se lo encargo Maestro, por favor cuidelo," (I leave him in your hands, please take care of him).

After I was informed of the incident, the mothers' words echoed for days. I thought of my own mother and father. It was evident that Silvio was one more casualty of the many who paid a huge price for acculturating into the urban lifestyle. He was another example of an American Dream who turned into an American Nightmare.

Practice What You Preach - Teach

Practice what you preach - teach was the message from Marvin, the quietest student in class. "Why would you stay here?" he said with a frown. "You should work for the United Nations. You should go do some of the things you talk to us about." His words triggered images of me at the United Nations speaking before representatives from all over the world. The images were soon overshadowed by thoughts of how difficult it would be to get my foot in the door. I would need to have the correct contacts and any other important details. Marvin's words reignited my passion to continue to fight a good fight. After all, I had spent an entire academic year thinking that Marvin was not paying attention to the lectures and class assignments, yet he was the one to encourage me to venture beyond the classroom and do exactly what I have been encouraging students to do all along.

Teaching is hard work – the politics, the rigid structure, the fading ability to be creative. It takes a toll! The past months have been extremely difficult and have affected my health in ways I could not have anticipated. As a result, I took more time off in three months than in the previous ten years. Marvin's words were profound and practical. His words were like a natural remedy and seemed to heal a lot of the cancerous energy that has chipped away at my being. Not only did I walk away from the conversation feeling a lot better, but determined to continue writing. Coincidentally, his words resonated and seemed to affirm an essay I was struggling to finish.

That evening for the first time in months, I began to write. The chattering inner voices that drove me crazy and prevented me from writing were dispelled and sent on a long vacation. It was then that I set forth to complete this essay. We know of stories in which teachers make a difference in the life of a student. Well in this case, it was a student who made a significant difference in the life of a teacher.

Do as I say not as I do seems to be the motto at most public schools. While teachers make requests of the students, we the teachers, seem to be of little to no example. In my eight years of working for the school district, I have been amazed to hear more about a principal's drinking habits than their philosophy on education and/or vision. How can we as a society, state, or nation expect better results from our schools when the leadership of our schools is known district-wide for their drinking habits and not for their vision or philosophy? Granted they are grown adults and are entitled to choosing how to live their lives. Regardless of their lifestyle, it should not overshadow their profession, their vision, or philosophy. A couple of years ago a colleague from a neighboring high school and I were discussing prom, then connected prom to drinking, to students being responsible, to faculty and administration chaperoning while boozing. I began to imagine a potential study on alcoholism and administration. I recall a major scandal that hit the press about administrators going to Las Vegas under the guise of employer paid conferences, and running up the taxpayers' tab. I do not recall anyone being held accountable for frivolous spending, yet administration is quick to write up a teacher for not having the "standard" written on the board?

This is no way to approach today's youth. Today's students may have low-test scores but they are neither blind nor are they naïve. Actually, I find that more students ask questions to test teachers than to fulfill an academic curiosity. Yet as adults, we continue to preach what we are not willing to practice as individuals or as a collective. We encourage, actually request, that students accept others despite difference of opinion, race, religion, gender, sexual preference, or lifestyle. This is under the auspices of tolerance, a word that is poorly used in trying to teach students to be accepting of others. Tolerance means acceptance, despite possible negative feelings or prejudices. At no point does tolerance invite the person to be open and understanding to differences. But even as the word tolerance is commonly and incorrectly used to promote understanding and equality among students, do teachers apply it themselves? The statement, "You're one of those," I often hear from colleagues in reaction to my teaching approach and ideologies. It is a sign of their disapproval of my questioning the functions of a school system. A few colleagues go as far as to badmouth me to students with their disapproval of my teaching philosophy. I imagine them cutting me down and criticizing me while paradoxically giving a lecture on accepting others.

What exactly will it take for teachers, like all other professionals, to practice what they preach? I recently encountered a heavyset woman eating at a fast food joint. She wore a name badge with the title, "Nutritionist." Certainly one must not be thin to be a nutritionist, but the content of what she was eating made me question the effectiveness of the message implied in her work to her clients. This reminded me of the many contradictions at school.

We preach abundance and tell students that they can accomplish anything they set their minds on – yet the district never has enough teachers, books, security guards, cafeteria food, money, or classrooms. Now there are excessive fundraising efforts by students for field trips. As a student, I never had to sell chocolates to go on a field trip. What happened in the last fifteen years that students must sell chocolates for field trips? The bigger question is, "When will the district have enough?" Not only do we preach having and living in abundance as a country, but we talk about the United States being the richest country in the world. If this is the case then why does the school district inadvertently promote so much scarcity and poverty?

As teachers we preach active participation yet most teachers practice silence and apathy. Afraid of retaliation most teachers do not speak up when they disagree with the administration. They are afraid their overtime will be taken away, their field trip will not be approved, their class will have no books, they will be assigned a remedial course (or even worse ESL), or simply that they will be given the silent treatment. Despite the teacher's silence, students are encouraged to ask questions, but only those that do not matter or challenge conventions of any sort. For example, students can ask for the name of Woodrow Wilson's wife, but cannot ask, "Why can't we have healthy food?" Students can ask, "Can I go to the restroom?" but cannot ask, "Contributions by Chicanos, Mexicans, and Central Americans missing in U.S. history textbooks, despite the U.S.'s constant interaction in Latin America?" Students can ask, "Was Hitler on antidepressants," but cannot ask, "Why are U.S. history books written with a White/Black paradigm? Students can ask the rhetorical question "Who killed JFK?" but not "Why do world history books mainly focus on Europe and the United States?" How would a teacher respond to a Latino or Chicano student if he or she were to ask, "If I matter as you say I do, why is my story not told in history books?"

It seems like high schools are not too different from colleges and universities. Throughout my college experience, I noticed a huge disconnect between academia and the real world. It seems that learning about a particular subject was one thing and applying the learned material to our everyday life was something completely different. It was not difficult to notice that some of the professors who stressed the importance of integration did not live in integrated communities. Ironically, they are the same people that talk about everybody getting along, yet they remove themselves from the environment where they would encounter having to get along with someone who is not like them. I had a professor who was a strong opponent of capitalism and fully embraced communism, yet he lived in the hills of Bel Air. He openly condemned the wealthy yet he surrounded himself with affluence. Noticing these contradictions made learning a bit confusing. I would sometimes question if learning within an academic institution was merely designed to stimulate conversation rather than put the learning's into practice.

When I understood the value of connecting the material learned in the classroom with the outside world, I made it a point to share personal stories and current events to facilitate that connection as a classroom teacher. One day, while I was gathering stacks of newspapers that I would take to the trash bin, I realized that the school district did not have a standard recycling system. I thought about the tons of paper that are thrown away on a weekly basis, none of which gets recycled. I then reflected on my own contradiction when I ask students to recycle. On a regular basis I reminded them to be efficient with everything they use: paper, water, aluminum, food, energy, and anything that has the potential of being wasted, including human energy. In essence, never take more than what you can give. Despite my lectures and conversations about recycling, I too was guilty of throwing away lots of recyclable paper on a regular basis. It hit me like a ton of bricks to realize that I worked for a school district that expected teachers to preach one thing, yet we practiced differently. As I thought of how irresponsible the district was being for not having a recycling system, I could not help noticing contradictions in other areas. I thought of how preaching one thing yet practicing another can be confusing for students who take much of what is said in the class as the final word and thus question very little.

Within minutes, I came up with an entire list of things that we as teachers, individually or as a collective district-wide, ignore. Far worse, most of us eagerly accept the status quo and provide little encouragement for students to question what we say and teach. Not only are we not teaching students to question, but we also are boldly telling them to conform. I have heard colleagues say, "Be happy you have a school to go to." "Be thankful you get a free meal, how many kids in Africa would not want to have a free lunch in school everyday?" While the intention is to have students appreciate their circumstances, the ultimate message is to conform and to not question. I am not sure that teachers would want students to say, "Stop complaining about your salary, teachers in Africa would love to earn a fraction of what you earn." I suppose a bigger question is, "Why is it that critical thought, by either teachers or students, is no longer accepted in public education?" Although I do not have an answer to the question, I can say that my memories of attending school are a bit different from what I see today. In general, I did not experience such a strong emphasis on taking a test that would not count for high school graduation.

Regardless of when the shift occurred or why it occurred, complete modeling of the curriculum is missing district-wide. "If I can only save one student," I have heard many colleagues say. Why would any teacher want to settle with only saving one student? I have asked myself this question a thousand times. Why can't we as teachers be as ambitious as we want our students to be? How would teachers view a student who stated, "If I can only pass one of my classes, I would be delighted?" My thought is that if you are aiming at only connecting with one student, you are in the wrong business. Can you imagine if the manager from a car dealer told his employees, "If you could sell at least one car, you've at least made one family happy."

Academic Rigor

The mission statement for San Fernando High School is one that promotes ambition for both learning and teaching. I suppose it is worth pointing out that it is not good enough to have a mission statement if it is not being carried out. More often than not students laugh when I read the mission statement to them in class. Their laughter is one of disbelief and cynicism. The mission Statement reads as follows:

> The San Fernando High School learning community is committed to offering a rigorous and relevant standards based curriculum, enabling our students to achieve academic excellence in a safe, supportive environment.

The idea of including the mission statement in this essay arose during a government class discussion. I asked the students to journal their thoughts on what democracy looks like. Only two out of twenty-nine felt comfortable in declaring that they knew what democracy was, but none of them could explain what democracy looks like. It was a reality check to observe how students have intellectualized the word democracy but are not able to explain democracy in practice. I pointed out to students that some of them might end up joining the military where they will be sent to Iraq to "establish democracy." Yet they do not know what it looks like at home. I wondered what the citizens of Iraq would think of the fact that high school seniors in the U.S. do not know what democracy looks like.

How can SFHS claim rigorous or academic excellence if the seniors cannot explain what democracy looks like? How can we continue to brag about having higher test scores if the students do not understand something that should be basic information, particularly in the U.S. where democracy is the essence of this nation? Yet, the district and the high school take much pride with the fact that test scores have increased.

How can students know what democracy looks like if they do not have a clear understanding of it? In their minds, democracy is associated with freedom and choices. Yet anyone who chooses to stand up and freely express themselves on the school campus, he or she will get labeled a troublemaker. Many of them remember the fact that students were cited for protesting. Many of them have witnessed administration harass me for encouraging students to think outside of the box or challenging the mechanics of the state standards movement within LAUSD. Most of them have given up on the idea that adults will consider and respect their opinion.

I continue to ask, what happened to rigor and academic excellence? Last academic year, upon receiving my new assignment, I found out that we had no textbooks for the bilingual world history course. The previous teacher, who was not credentialed to teach the course and was the *compadre* of the former principal had been handing out translated chapter summaries. This was acceptable for the teacher and administration. Last year while covering classes during my conference period I realized that other classes did not have a textbook. How is it possible that entire classes start their academic year without a textbook?

What is rigorous about only offering Spanish as a foreign language in a school where 90 percent of the student body already speak the language? What is rigorous about having a sports program that cannot get any of the star players into a four-year university?

At the beginning of the fourth week of school, when first quarter grades are due, students are still shuffled around to balance the classes. If this happened once, it would not be worth writing about, but this is a yearly occurrence that is accepted by the faculty. Administration expects students to be ready the first day of class, yet they are not ready for the students. In my second period government course, an overwhelming majority of the students had their classes switched around a minimum of three times during the first three weeks of the semester. The most affected were the seniors who are expected to apply to college, prepare for the SAT, and deal with the pressures of being a senior. Yet they still had to adjust their schedule one quarter later. Some students went from geometry to algebra while others went from economics to government. With the different styles, pace, and expectations of teachers, how long would it take before students settle in and adapt to their new schedule? By then we will be entering the midterm progress report card and administrators will be blaming teachers as to why we are not communicating with parents about their child's progress. Yet administration will never acknowledge that students are behind due to a bad start and poor administrative planning. Administrators are great at selectively holding teachers accountable, and even better at justifying their poor leadership.

I have several fifth year seniors, also known as super seniors, who are behind in credits, yet their counselor assigns them a service class – teaching assistantship. I have a young lady who is a senior yet can barely speak English; she was given a service class instead of an academic course that would support her in improving her English. If these stories were in isolation, it would not be worth mentioning, but these stories are commonplace and repeat themselves year in and out.

What is so rigorous about giving students Regional Opportunity Program (ROP) credits to graduate? ROP is a work program where students spend a certain number of hours at a work location and receive credits towards graduation. Ideally, ROP serves as an apprenticeship where students learn job related skills and the intricacies of running the business. The reality is that students become volunteers or free labor for major department stores like Wal-Mart. Personally it sounds like another form of indentured servitude: students have to work hours in exchange for high school credits. Why would a school agree to send students to a company that has a bad history of low wages with poor to no benefits? Students have shared that they are being assigned to work regular tasks (e.g. stocking, maintenance, warehouse, etc.) and are never instructed on how to operate an aspect of the business. Certainly if it was known that students in China were receiving high school credits for working in factories it would be condemned as child labor and the U.S. government would be requesting that China put an end to such practices.

Another example of the contradiction between the mission statement and student expectations is the fact that students are allowed to fail up to two courses and still play sports as long as they can maintain a 2.0 grade point average (GPA). In addition, district policy states that teachers must accept all late work as long as students clear their absence. Clearly, the district turns a blind eye to the massive forgery of notes. Finally, the district accepts the fact that the average graduating senior is reading at a ninth grade level (this has not changed since I graduated 15 years ago). Worse, I have watched documentaries on the Civil Rights Movement that provide a similar figure. So if the average reading rate has not improved in over 50 years, what changes have been made? It is easy for critics to blame undocumented students, but research shows that even predominantly White suburban schools are also having a problem with graduation and reading rates.

SFHS, is a microscopic example of the systemic problem within the district and possibly the nation. It is clearly not modeling the rigor and or high academic excellence that it purports. Yet the district expects students to increase scores, graduate, and go to college under the condition of low to no expectations. The learning environment is so depressed that I have yet to meet a teacher who is brave enough to enroll his/her son or daughter into regular public school. It is important that I specify regular schools because we have a handful that have enrolled their teens in the magnet program.

Health

The curriculum taught in class is one that promotes "a healthy lifestyle." We highly encourage students to hydrate themselves and have a nutritious diet in order to have a healthy lifestyle. The district went as far as to eliminate vending machines with sodas and junk food. Recently, the district changed their flexible policies and is now requiring that all students take Physical Education (P.E.) class and will no longer permit dance classes or cheerleading to count for P.E. While some of these changes may come across as a step in the right direction, what is the district actually modeling?

When I was in elementary, the school had student workers (cafeteria monitors) who assisted in the food preparation on campus. Today all the food is processed and are supplied by outside vendors. Students constantly complain about expired milk. To add insult to injury, there is nothing healthy about the usual greasy pizza or the dry hamburgers with its precisely cut single piece of lettuce. Even worse, in a year-round and overcrowded school like SFHS, there are only twenty-nine minutes allotted to feed over 3,500 students, faculty, and staff. By the time students go to their locker, wash their hands, and stand in line, seven to nine minutes have passed. They stand in line for an additional five to seven minutes. After eating they literally have eight minutes before they must head to the restroom to wash their hands and or take care of personal necessities. If a student were to stay after class to clarify something from the lecture, that student could run the risk of not having lunch or being late to their next class. Because this system is one that students are too familiar with, no real digestion takes place and few students actually wash their hands before and after lunch. They arrive to class wired from whatever they ate or drank during lunch. Although the junk food vending machines have been eliminated, students sell junk food all day in order to raise funds for clubs and/or sports programs. I have counted as many as eight students in a single class selling Hot Cheetos, caramel apples, lollipops, car wash tickets, raffle tickets, key chains, T-shirts, and other things. I have jokingly told students that they are being prepared to be street vendors.

In exploring the topic of food and diet I realized that most of my former teachers were overweight. I never gave it much thought until now. At this point, I am not sure if it is the cafeteria food; teachers eat the same food that students eat. My stomach tends to blow up every time that I eat cafeteria food for a long period of time. When I made that observation I cut back on cafeteria food in general and began buying more salads and fruits.

The district preaches healthy lifestyles yet cannot accommodate a basic need, a healthy meal. There is curriculum on health at all levels of education and even have workshops for parents, but the district cannot provide a healthy meal. How hypocritical is that? The school district tells parents how to feed their children, and then do the exact opposite when the children are under their custody. The movie "Supersize Me" clearly underscores this issue by comparing meals at two different institutions. The first is a public school where students eat cafeteria food. The second is a continuation school where students eat homemade food. The result from this comparison is mind blowing.

Environment

"Do as I say not as I do," is a common statement that adults say to the youth. As a society, we seem to embrace this credo. It is most obvious in our homes when alcoholic parents tell their children not to drink. Or parents who consciously give up fighting for a quality life tell their children to strive for more. Both are examples of situations from which parents learned from their decisions and want their children to create something different by benefiting from their hard-learned lessons.

Over the years I have come to value and appreciate the natural environment. I went as far as selling my all-time favorite vehicle, a blue Chevy truck. It had an altered engine that polluted the air as much as a factory from the 1900s. I bought the truck long before I had developed awareness for the care of the environment and had no understanding of how I was personally affecting Mother Earth. I have made behavioral changes with the products I purchase, recycling, and minding how I use water and energy. I continue to be mindful of areas that need improvement. I will not take from the environment more than what I give. While I constantly reflect on human behavior, I cannot pretend that my habits at work are in accord at home. At school every time that I throw away what should be recyclable paper, I am reminded that there is no recycling system for the tons of paper that go to waste, daily, monthly, and, on a yearly basis. More scandalous is that students litter the floor with food and paper with no regard for the environment or concern for the cleanliness of school campus. As they unconsciously walk down the hallway they carelessly drop things they no longer want. If you bring it to their attention, they will interpret the reprimand as an overreaction by an adult. Their attitude is nonchalant and uncaring. I have come to understand that students are following the adults who model throwing away paper in the trash instead of recycling. As a teacher, I might argue that I have no choice in throwing the paper in the regular trashcan and place the blame on the administration or the district. The reality is that administration and the district are also unaware of their behavior; everyone is on autopilot. In the case of the recycling system, few seem to be asking where the tons of should-be-recycled-paper goes.

I am certain that there are a handful of individual schools that have mediocre to great recycling systems. Unfortunately, most schools do not have any basic recycling program in place, making it difficult to actually argue that the district is doing something about it. Two months after I began writing this essay SFHS's student government created a recycling system for the campus. They set up containers throughout the cafeteria for students to dispose their plastic bottles and or aluminum cans. Three months later the project was terminated for its lack of use by the students, teachers, and administration alike.

Life Long Learners

The idea of "life long learners" is a catchy three-word phrase that tends to be a common phrase used in faculty meetings. It is profound by proclamation, noble in nature, but loosely used by administration. Oftentimes I wonder if administration uses such academic jargon to impress faculty; to make us think that they know what they are doing. The idea of creating life long learners should be status quo, but how can we create life long learners? The essence of life long learners is a student who never stops learning; a student who falls in love with the act of learning; a student who chooses to learn for the sake of learning. Yet how can our students be life long learners when many adults who are outdated in their thinking and pedagogical approach surround them, and are not open to change? We laugh when we hear about a person who still listens to an eight-track or cassette tape and refuse to upgrade to CD, or better yet an iPod. Yet the reality in schools is far sadder than someone who refuses to change and give up an outdated eight-track or cassette deck. A high percentage of teachers are afraid of modern technology and few are abreast of the latest research in their respective discipline. These teachers are as outdated as the person who still uses an eight-track. The question then becomes, how can we as a district expect students to be life long learners if faculty and staff are not willing to be life long learners? The amount of complaining for having to attend professional development is extraordinarily high. The percentage of teachers who are afraid to use the internet is even higher.

Whether or not the teachers are technologically savvy, the amount of avenues for students to get the credits they need is vast. Last year all social studies teachers were trained to facilitate "Service Learning Projects," a new graduation requirement. The project is supposed to be student led and designed for students to experience project-based research. Students are expected to document the entire learning process and divide the work amongst their classmates. The concept of the Service Learning Project is great, however, in practice the implementation is a separate reality. This past year Principal Mr. Rail approved student participation in City of Los Angeles Mayor Antonio Villaraigosa's Day of Service for Service Learning credits. The Day of Service is a citywide event where the Mayor calls all city residents to volunteer on a community project, whether it is cleaning streets, planting trees, or retouching a mural. During the Service Learning training provided by the school it was made clear that the basis of the project is not to volunteer, rather for students to go through the motions of creating their own project. At SFHS, many students were essentially given credits for volunteering to clean the school for a couple of hours and write an essay about their experience.

Before the principal approved the City of Los Angeles' Day of Service as a legitimate Service Learning Project all of my seniors had selected an actual service learning project. The minute it became known that the principal had approved Day of Service, all but three students dropped the original project. A senior from another class joined them. These four students collected data on local cement skate parks, developed a power point presentation, collected over one-thousand signatures from students and community members, made phone calls to local elected officials, and presented their project before the Commission of Recreation and Community Services in the City of San Fernando. Their hard work became publicly known when their story was published in a local newspaper.

What is the fundamental role of schools, if they are not willing to practice what they preach? In recent years, it feels as if my role is only to teach test-taking strategies and trivial knowledge. A huge emphasis is placed on test scores and little to no effort is given to human relations, increasing graduation rates, or improving attendance. Administration has forgotten that the average high school graduate is reading at a ninth grade level. Focusing on higher scores while ignoring to teach students the basics is like qualifying a racehorse for its beauty without regard of its speed.

Why I Teach

Over the years many students have asked me, "Why did you decide to become a teacher?" I have never been able to answer their question without sharing life experiences. As much as I attempted to share everything, every time I have answered this question my story continued expanding. By the time I was done relating a memory or experience, I realized that I could have shared a little more. Their question compelled me to continue exploring my personal and profound reason why I decided to teach, despite never having been a dedicated student and not caring about education when I was their age. That was true until I started college. The more I explored the question, the more I realized that there is no one specific reason. A series of life experiences are what brought me back to the same institution that I was so desperate to leave only years earlier. These same life experiences are what made my tenure with LAUSD a bittersweet journey.

It was my first semester in college when I realized that I wanted to teach at the high school level. I came to that realization after taking four very distinct classes. Up until that point, I was confused and did not have a clue as to what I would do with my life. I was certain of one thing, to prove wrong everyone who underestimated me. I needed to prove something to the college advisor from Monroe High School because he advised me to attend North Valley Occupational Center and learn how to paint cars. I needed to prove to my parents that I could break the traditional expectations, namely getting a high school diploma, help the family, save money, buy a car, buy a house, get married, and eventually live the same life as everyone before me. I needed to prove to my brother who thought, and continues to think, that he is the only scholar in the family. I needed to prove to my counselor who would not let me take a biology class because "this is a college prep course that requires advanced math and you are only in pre-algebra." I needed to prove to all of the homeboys that we could change our lifestyle and contribute positive things to the world. I needed to prove to the racist White people who I had personally encountered in my life that I would not spend the rest of my life in a labor-intensive job making them rich. Most of all, I needed to prove to myself that I could succeed in school if I gave myself permission and opportunity to do so.

One of the four classes that I took my first semester in college was Fire Science. I tried hard to convince myself that I wanted to be a fire fighter. This notion to convince myself was an attempt to avoid spending four years in college. Initially, my confusion about having to select a career led me to research several careers that did not require a college degree. I obviously was looking for a quick solution to the popular question "What will I do with the rest of my life?" Since I had convinced myself that I did not like school and was not good in school, I looked at jobs with the fire department, police department, sheriffs, as well as other city jobs. As I researched the pros and cons it didn't take long for me to realize that they were all dead end jobs where I would be limited for having only a high school diploma – not to mention I was extremely insecure about my low level of reading and writing. During this time Rodney King was brutally beat by the Los Angeles Police Department officers. Racism, which I had encountered as a teenager, was now visible to the public via television and became manifested on a grand scale. After seeing the beating and then hearing the public commentary supporting the police officers, I decided not to associate myself with this department so I immediately scratched law enforcement off the list. To make matters worse, a few of my homeboys and I were humiliated and eventually assaulted a few months after the Rodney King incident. (Although we had many eyewitnesses, everyone's video cameras were at home.) A week after the incident occurred, my father took me to the emergency room at midnight as a result of a horrible migraine headache. The doctors told me that I had a sprained jaw. That injury was a result of an officer placing his knee on my back while I was hand cuffed and lying on the ground. He slammed my face onto the concrete. He did this because I turned my head around to ask him a question. I filed a grievance with LAPD and the conclusion of the investigation found the officers to be innocent from any wrongdoing. The force used upon me was "necessary to ensure the officer's safety," as it was concluded. Thereafter, I decided that I could not work for an organization that I resented so much. Actually, it was more than resentment. It was hatred. I hated them with a passion for their abusive way of handling teenagers and people of color. The police go out of their way "to teach us a lesson." I am sure that their "lesson" wore on them more (than what they intended to teach us). I imagined they went home and took it out on their wives, pets, or drank themselves to misery. I had also thought about joining the Marines to get money for college. I then noticed that most of the guys who joined never went to college. On top of that, I was not feeling too patriotic about putting up with some redneck yelling at me to do pushups. I was yelled at enough as a teenager. I did not care to be yelled at as a young adult.

I played with one idea after another only to realize that I did not want to be a firefighter. I eventually dropped the class two weeks into the semester. I also realized that I was too young not to be in school and to work full-time for the rest of my life. I finally decided that I would stay in college and do things differently.

The second class I took was drafting. I had taken an introduction course in architecture and advanced drafting courses in high school. The college professor appreciated my work and recommended me to his friend who needed someone to create blue prints for lamps. I went to the interview and was offered the job only to realize that I would be working alone in a cubicle. The thought of not having someone to talk to drove me crazy. The job was on a contractual basis and I was not guaranteed continuous employment. I did not care to have a job that lacked ongoing financial stability. Despite the decent salary, I turned down the job. I finished the class and concluded that I would not be able to handle a job in that profession.

Somewhere between high school and community college I began to consider being a probation officer. I am not sure why. Many of my homeboys were on probation and only spoke negative things about the probation department. Without ever being on probation, their stories had convinced me that probation officers were equally abusive as cops. As I played with the idea of being a probation officer, I realized that I could not work for a department who was hated by the people they served. Yet, I still had an interest in the subject so I took a Sociology class on juvenile delinquency. It was not the content of the class that further sparked my interest in Sociology, but the professor. I had never met a White lady as crazy and challenging as her. Patricia Lenin, a feminist, communist, and atheist. This crazy lady turned out to be one of the best professors I ever had. Her class was intense and she challenged every belief that I had. Professor Lenin was not afraid to get loud and in my face, if that was required of her to get the point across. The topics of discussion were stimulating and got me to think more about working with youth, just not as a probation officer.

I took another Sociology course, which I eventually dropped as a result of the requirements. The class consisted of doing community service through an organization called Friends Outside, a nonprofit that assisted convicts and family members in locating each other. Some of them lost contact as a result of being transferred from one prison to another. For others it was the opposite, the family would move and addresses would get lost. I was surprised to hear of family members who also lost contact and purposefully distanced themselves from the inmate. I could not stop thinking of the many homeboys I knew who were in prison. During a field trip to the Sybil Brand Institute, Los Angeles County woman's jail, I asked the officer if I could look up a homeboy in their system: their system was connected to all detention facilities within the state. I could not believe that I was able to find his location in the massive penal system! I also could not believe what I saw during the fieldtrip. The biggest shock came in the maternity section – all of the inmates were pregnant. Growing up I had never thought about women in prison, much less pregnant women. I also saw an old woman lie on a concrete bed with a thin mattress, which appeared to me as her deathbed. I could not think of a reason as to why an old woman, who reminded me of my grandmother, was incarcerated. She was neither in the special unit with the killers nor was she wearing the bright orange jump suit that would have identified her as not qualified to post bail. What could this old woman have done to spend her last days in county jail? Seeing women in prison brought images of all of the women in my life – my grandmother, mother, sister, aunts, cousins, girlfriends, and coworkers. Growing up I only knew of guys going in and out of juvenile hall, county jail, and eventually hard prison – not women.

The fourth and final class was a Chicano Studies course. The professor was Dr. Miranda, the first Chicana with a doctoral degree that I had ever met. Actually, she was the first minority that I had met with a doctoral degree. She introduced herself eloquently and made every word count when she spoke. As I sat in class listening to her lectures, I wondered why we did not have professionals like her in high school. I loved to hear her properly pronounce Spanish words while mixing them up with the English language.

She actually rolled her R's when pronouncing a word in Spanish. Gutierrez was Gutierrez and not Goo-dee-air-ehs, Goot-tair-es or Goo-teh-rehz. By hearing her pronounce my name in Spanish, as it should be, I learned that it was okay to be bilingual and properly pronounce Spanish when speaking it. Furthermore, it was okay to be Mexican. For me that was very insightful because until then, I had been fighting to keep my name intact from having it butchered by White teachers who consistently tried to call me Al, or Albert. Although I never allowed my name to be butchered, I did mispronounce it, Anglicizing it to please monolingual English speakers: Alberto became Al-burr-toe. My uncle Jesus would make fun of how I pronounced my name and called me Al-burro. Damn I hated having him make fun of me, but deep down inside I knew he was right. I sounded like a fool as I made futile attempts to please people who did not speak Spanish or those who were embarrassed to speak Spanish.

Along the way many high school buddies called me "Berto." I was cool with it, because it did not sound as White as Al or Albert. To make things easier I always preferred to go by Beto. I figured White people would have no way to Anglicize and distort Beto, which is a shorter version of Alberto. It took a while but they finally managed to distort it: Bay-toe, Bee-toe, and Bay-doe with an occasional Bethel, sometimes it even sounded like beetle. Although teachers would praise bilingualism, I think they were referring to Italian, French or any other European language. Associating Spanish with immigration, Latin America, Mexico more specifically, it was just not as "classy" for them, or so I thought. I remember hearing teachers struggle to pronounce words in French or Italian properly, but it was not as important to do so in Spanish. As a student I could never understand why students would learn a European language if they had no one with whom to speak outside of class. The overwhelming majority of them would probably never even visit Europe.

In this Chicano Studies class I came to realize that if I would have been taught a history that was inclusive and embraced my history during my primary and secondary education, I most likely would not have taken school lightly, nor would I have gotten involved in gangs. It was rejuvenating to learn about a U.S. history that began in the west coast and not in the east coast with the 13 colonies. Learning all of this information late in my education made it so that I had to re-learn everything that I was taught. Columbus was really an assassin who wiped out the Taino people, and set the foundation for other European explorers to participate in the extinction of indigenous people of the Americas. Yet he continues to be praised as an explorer and was given a national holiday. Putting things into perspective, Christopher Columbus killed more people and set the stage for millions more to be killed within the Americas than Hitler, Saddam Hussein, and Osama Bin Ladin combined. Yet Columbus is praised as a hero, but why? Students know more about the holocaust than their own history of the Americas. I was overwhelmed with learning about the many historical figures that were omitted from U.S. history textbooks. It was fascinating to learn the story behind the names of so many cities and streets that are in Spanish, right here in California, Los Angeles, San Fernando Valley. Columbus opened the doors for the Spanish crown, killed and massacred so many indigenous people, and also gave birth to a lot of history that I came to appreciate. I suppose a big contradiction would be ignoring what really took place over 500 years ago when Columbus first arrived. While today we cannot change the outcome of the massacred indigenous people of the Americas, nor can we reverse the committed atrocities, we should not prohibit the truth from being told.

After taking the Chicano Studies course, the name Pacoima was no longer only a poverty-stricken gang infested city. Pacoima was the name given by the Tongva people who were the first inhabitants of the region, and means "The Entrance." I began to see Pacoima as being rich with history and culture, despite the high unemployment rate, the liquor stores on every corner, and the gang problems. Years later, I read *Hoyt Street* by Mary Helen Ponce and life in Pacoima was restored. I was raised being afraid and embarrassed of Pacoima as a direct result of all of the negative comments made by teachers. My seventh and eighth grade P.E. teacher referred to Pacoima as the armpit of the Valley and constantly threatened to transfer us to their junior high school for misbehaving.

The name Pico was more than a street that crossed the City of San Fernando. It was the name of the last person to Govern California under Mexican rule. Pio Pico was his complete name, but most of us who see the street never knew about Pio, only Pico. Most drive onto Pico or through Pico without questioning the name. Some of the homies might even have it tattooed on their stomach, eyebrow, neck, lip, earlobe, knuckles or any other visible place. Sadly, the overwhelming majority of them do not know the story behind the territory that they claim.

In learning about history that I identified with, I gained a sense of self worth. I also understood why the U.S. government would not want to teach a comprehensive history in primary or secondary schools. What would the government do if the majority of the minority grew up knowing an accurate history that actually validated them as human beings, and not as members of a minority group?

Instead, little to no history was taught about people of color, making it seem as if we made little to no contribution to history. To keep everyone quiet, U.S. History books have taken one or two members of each minority group and commercialized their story and image. People like Cesar Chavez and Martin Luther King Jr. are both great examples. I often ask if we have no other hero outside of Cesar Chavez. In the early 90s, Cesar Chavez was not as known as he is today, yet despite only focusing on the organization of farm workers I remember that he was like a spokesperson for the entire community. Why go to a farm worker organizer to ask him about events happening in the city? Do we not have anyone in the city who could answer the question? More than ten years after his death, schools talk about Chavez as if he is the only hero for the Chicano/Latino community. People like World War II veteran Guy Gabaldon, who single handedly captured over 1,000 prisoners of war without having to kill anyone, and had a movie (Hell to Eternity, starring Jeffrey Hunter) made after his heroic work, is not mentioned in high school US history books. With the ongoing wars and killing of hundreds of thousands of innocent people, why would the U.S. Government teach students about a guy who went to war and received a medal for capturing so many prisoners without killing them? Then there is Pedro

Gonzalez, the founder of the first Spanish radio station in Los Angeles. He spent six years in San Quentin on trumped-up charges for using the radio to organize the Mexican community during the great depression. The movie *Break of Dawn* was a portrayal of his heroic effort. Far worse, Mexicanas/Chicanas and Latin American woman in general are rarely mentioned. At one point, I was given a set of posters that represented diversity and the late singer Selena was one of them. As much as I acknowledge her struggle as an up and coming singer, she was never an established person who spoke for the community. United States History textbooks continue to overlook the contributions that Mexicana/Chicana and or women from Latin America make. The story of Loretta Velazquez, a Cuban born woman whose Spanish father was granted an estate in Texas just before the Mexican-American War, is a classic example. Loretta was obsessed with the war and joined the Confederate army after marrying a southerner. She disguised herself, adopted the name of Lieutenant H.T. Bufford, C.S.A., and joined the Civil War. She fought in major battles, eventually got wounded, and also met President Abraham Lincoln. It's a shame that history books are written in such a way that Mexicans don't exist during certain time periods.

How would Black students react to history if they learned that the Texas Revolt, which eventually led to the Mexican American War, was the result of Mexico prohibiting slavery to White settlers? This made me wonder how Black students in high school would react if they knew that Mexico defended the rights of slaves long before Abraham Lincoln signed the Emancipation Proclamation. Would we have had so many race riots if both groups understood how intertwined our history is? Would we have the tension in prisons or on the street if Blacks and Mexicanos/Chicanos/Centro Americanos understood how much we all have in common? I was shocked to find out that runaway slaves would cross the border into Mexico. "When did that happen?" I frequently asked myself in disbelief. But it made sense. For many slaves in the Deep South, the Mexican border was closer than the free northern states. Unfortunately, high school students continue to be taught that all runaway slaves ventured towards the north. Would we continue to have so much racial tension between Brown and Black students in high schools if a comprehensive history was taught? It is clear to me that most of these race riots were a matter of misunderstanding.

Throughout high school, I sensed that something was wrong with history. It seemed like everything was White or Black. Whites sat in the front of the bus and Blacks sat in the back of the bus. "Where were we sitting?" I would silently ask myself. Maybe we did not have a seat and had to stand up. Is it possible that we were driving the bus, or maybe walking alongside it? Either way, little to no mention was given about Mexicans. But that was odd, considering California was governed by Mexico, and streets and cities everywhere are in Spanish. "How can we not be mentioned in history books?"

Chicano studies introduced me to a profound layer of racism, one that is not physically visible and is widely ignored. Racism, as I had learned about it in high school disappeared the day the signs were taken down. Students and society at large tend to identify racism with the physical signs that read, "NO Mexicans and NO Dogs Allowed" "NO Beaners, Greasers or Spicks" or "Colored Only" "NO Negro" or "NO Niggers" and "White Only." Being that these signs are no longer publicly visible, high school students, who are a microcosm of society, believe that racism is no longer real and rampant. A common remark that I grew up hearing is, "the country is not ready for a Black president." Yet the concept of having a Chicano/Latino President was never even a remote consideration.

The process of equality began when the courts struck down the practice of separate but equal and forced integration to take place in all public and many private sectors. With time, additional policy was created to eradicate open discrimination and the abolishment of the physical signs of racism. This is the time period which we live in, no signs hang anywhere that openly discriminate based on race, religion, or gender. Generally speaking, our ahistorical, apolitical society tends to associate racism with a practice of the past; a practice that ended with the assassination of Martin Luther King Jr., or the forced integration post Brown v. Board of Topeka Kansas decision. When I mention the concept of racism in class, most students see it as a thing of the past. Racism is associated as only a Black/White dichotomy. By the end of the semester, many students have expressed major internal conflict for their newfound discovery of the world they thought they lived in and the one that they learn about through the course of their newfound awareness. Two years ago, the administration wrote me up for integrating the Mexican history that books tend to omit. The students witnessed it all. It turned out to be the best present day example. The day after students took the California Standardized Test (CST), Natalia, a student in one of my U.S. history classes, mentioned how only one question was asked about Mexican-US History. According to Natalia, the question was associated with Cesar Chavez (no surprise), the correct answer was Cesar Chavez (no surprise) and the alternative answers were all Black historical figures (no surprise). She laughed in disbelief as she shared her observation in class. I explained how her observation was a sign of major growth, the ability to see the world through the lens of a Mexicana. Natalia's observation makes sense. The US history books have no other prominent Mexicano/Chicano/Centro Americano leaders who could be used as alternative answers when asking a question about Cesar Chavez.

Entering community college exposed me to so much information that I felt the need to take it back to the high schools. The more I learned, the more I was convinced that I would have chosen a different path had I been exposed in high school to the wealth of knowledge I was exposed to at the community college. By the end of the first semester, I decided to become a high school teacher. I constantly thought of my homeboys and wealth of knowledge they were missing. Upon enrolling at Los Angeles Valley College (LAVC) I convinced one of my homeboys to join me. We both took the Sociology as well as the Chicano Studies course. After class, we would go to his house to do our homework, something that was completely new to me, and together we struggled to understand the texts. It took us a good three hours to read and comprehend one paragraph. We would read, reread, and reread, write in the margins, circle words, underline parts of sentences until we understood the material. Even then, we were never sure if we understood, since we had no immediate way of checking.

A month or so into our journey he disappeared for a few days. Soon enough I found out that our rival gang had shot him in the neck. Brown against Brown never made sense, but after exploring Chicanos Studies, it especially did not make sense. I grappled with visiting him at the hospital but eventually went. While at the hospital, I remember talking more with his mother than with him. I was resentful that he could not maintain the discipline needed to stay away from the neighborhood, as we had said we would do. I was at a crossroad, one where I found myself having to choose between personal transformation, committing to change the educational system, or maintaining my relationship with childhood friends. The decision was tough but I knew I would not be able to do all three. As it was, my past continued to haunt me and I was aware that old enemies would not turn a blind eye if they saw me in public. In fact, because some of our enemies were also attending the same community college, my homeboy and I would take a gun to school in our backpack. To lessen the crime he carried the gun and I carried the clip with the bullets. In retrospect, it was ridiculous for us to feel the need to carry a gun to school, but that was our reality and experience.

By the end of the first semester, my thoughts had evolved more than I was able to handle at times. Occasionally I found myself torn between who I was and the person I aspired to be. I wanted to shake off my past and start fresh, but that was impossible. I would condemn my past, my present, and God. What did I do to deserve this? I would ask the empty skies. Why did you pull me out of the neighborhood into a world that was far colder and full of so many unknowns? I became hungrier to comprehend the details that made the world turn. I began to read in order to improve my reading skills and catch up with my peers who seemed to have read a lot more during their high school years. The more I read, the more anxious I became to return and share the information with teenagers.

I was technically still a high school student when I started my first semester in college. Because I had attended summer school every year I had accumulated enough credits to finish one semester early. The school allowed me to return for the graduation ceremony. That first semester in college I joined M.E.Ch.A. (Movimiento Estudiantil

Chicanos de Aztlan), a student organization whose birth can be traced to the 1960's Civil Rights, Chicano Movement. This group of Mechistas became my base of support and good friends. Through M.E.Ch.A. I met other young idealists who understood my personal struggle. It was then that I first left Los Angeles (without it being a trip to visit my grandparents in Mexico). I had the privilege to attend conferences in Santa Fe, Nuevo Mexico, as well as Davis and Fresno, California. I had never felt as free in my life. I had no worries nor concern of having to look over my shoulder. I did not have to be on the defensive. Attending a conference with hundreds of educated brown females and males was an experience beyond what any words could describe. I still get the chills when I think of the discussions that took place and the camaraderie that we shared.

Shortly after the end of my first semester in college, I read Malcolm X's autobiography. He had something that I wanted. I was not exactly sure what it was, but I wanted whatever Malcolm was offering me at the time. I became immediately absorbed by his struggle and drew many parallels of his story with my experience. A lot of my thoughts of racism and White supremacy were spelled out clearly by Malcolm X. The poor schooling that I was subjected to by LAUSD was an example of the systemic racism of our times. I frequently thought about the homies and wondered what they would think of Malcolm X's interpretation of racism. Would they share my reaction or would they see him as another *mayate* (derogatory term used by Latinos in reference to Blacks) and completely discredit his message for being? In some ways it did not matter, most of my homies did not fully understand the transformation that I was experiencing. Going to college was more than taking classes and getting a grade. At times, I would wake up and physically feel the intellectual growth within me. This strange feeling of intellectual growth would suddenly take my sleep or tiredness away and I would sit and ponder on how I could have been strategic in the class debate that took place the day before. Aside from the constant personal growth came a feeling of responsibility to take this knowledge back to as many youngsters as possible. Maybe they would be able to avoid the many pitfalls into which I had fallen. By now, I saw or considered knowledge in textbooks as instruments to initiate a change, especially the change that I envisioned for the world. It was not much different from the discussed ideas in Chicano Studies or Sociology. It was no different from some of the ideas proposed by Malcolm X.

Unlike Malcolm X, I was never physically imprisoned, but I felt a sense of imprisonment within a society that was full of contradictions. This society cared more about image and control than integrity and real freedom. I lived in a society that preached democracy but did not know how to practice it. To practice democracy and speak up made you an unpatriotic and ungrateful citizen living in the best country of the world.

When I began to teach in public schools, I naively believed that an interest in educating youth existed and I would be able to contribute. I soon realized that public schools mastered the art of mass production of functional illiterates and were not teaching any critical thinking. Everything revolved around test scores. The longer I stayed with the district the easier it was for me to understand why I grew up not liking school. Everything seemed to revolve around test scores and standardized thinking, and a continuous stream of promotions for administrators.

Being that my first teaching assignment was at my alma mater, it was only a matter of time before I bumped into former teachers who had written me off during my high school years. Football Coach Putz was one the first people I bumped into when I first began my assignment. He still seemed to be upset at the fact that I quit my senior year, along with a couple of other players. He was such a racist that we opted not to play for him. We even heckled the team from the stands. One day, after losing another student, Coach Putz was so pissed at us for heckling the team that he jumped one of the gates and challenged me to jump the other gate. The old man wanted to fight me. I laughed at him and his theatrics. Within seconds of jumping the fence, he yelled from the top of his lungs, "You're the biggest jerk on this campus Goo-di-erez!" Now we were face to face in the office and I was his colleague. He would now address me as Mr. Gutierrez or I could address him as Bob. I felt empowered seeing this man walk miserably through the halls, just as he did when I was a student. I bumped into other former teachers; most could not look at me in the eye and congratulate me for such radical transformation. I remind them of how badly they mistreat and underestimate their students. Only a very small number of teachers congratulated me. Among them were the same teachers who encouraged me when I was a student.

At the age of 23, I looked very young and was often mistaken for a student. It took a couple of years for faculty and staff to stop confusing me for a student. Oftentimes, I was treated rudely, yelled at, and kicked out of offices. I was once asked to hang up the phone while attempting to contact a parent of one of my students. The experience served as a reminder of what it was like to be a student of color in high school. Most teachers had little to no respect for students and I was personally experiencing their hostility even though I was their peer. One day I was playing handball after school with some students. I hit the ball over the wall and into the tennis courts then went to retrieve it. I waved my hands in the air and signaled a student on the tennis team to throw me the ball. Before the student could act on my request, the tennis coach, who was also the Department Chair for Social Studies, snatched the ball from the student and hit it with his racket as far as possible into the soccer fields. The students with whom I was playing handball noticed and immediately looked at me. Their eyes were full of mixed emotions and although none of them said a word, their eyes conveyed the stories of their sad thoughts. It was obvious that this was not the first time this teacher had behaved in such a manner. When I read the faces of the students, I also knew that they wanted me to speak up, something that few teachers had done for them. They knew that his aggression was aimed at them, the ESL students, and not at me, another teacher. The attitude would have been different if it was a baseball or a football – generally speaking ESL students don't play either sport. I felt compelled to say something, but did not want to stoop to his level. I simply called him by name and stated, "Thank you, I will have the soccer team get the ball for us." He turned as red as possible, realizing that his true self was blatantly transparent and his tennis players were all staring at him.

The next day in class, I had a discussion with the students about respect, something that few teachers gave the students. To a huge degree nothing had changed from when I was a student. The racism was simply more subtle. There I was defending ESL students, just as I had done when I was in school.

When I started teaching and thinking about my time in school, I realized that I was a student in public school during a period with many historical events but never knew of their importance. I realized this as an adult when I became a teacher and read for pleasure and curiosity. I read on historical events like the Nelson Mandela trials, the wars in Central America, and the invasion of Panama. Because the school textbooks did not mention these events, teachers did not talk about them. It seemed like books only validated the French and American Revolution, all other revolutions were overlooked and or not given the same importance (e.g. the Mexican, Cuban, and Haitian revolutions). It is interesting how revolutionary heroes are mentioned and positioned in U.S. history books like George Washington and Fidel Castro. Washington was a slave owner, yet he is praised for his victory against the British. Fidel Castro on the other hand took an interest in educating Black Cubans and providing them with the equality they never had prior to the Cuban Revolution. Yet Fidel is known as a dictator and blamed for the existing poverty of Cuba. No positive acknowledgement is given to him for his victory over Fulgensio Batista's oppressive dictatorship. High school history books will not acknowledge the effects of the U.S. embargo on the small island of Cuba. Both revolutions were led by great leaders yet history books do not recognize the struggle of revolutions that do not benefit "American interests." These are some examples of written history not being neutral.

Today, I reflect on these observations because the district continues to push for the standardization of all material and its alignment to the state test. I was told, "If it is not in the state test, don't teach it. Let's focus only on information that will count." As a result, most of today's youth are disconnected from current world events that affect their everyday lives. This is why I teach and love history. I strive to bridge the gap of knowledge and provide students with a comprehensive approach to the material that explains our existence on earth, who we are, where we come from, and where we are going.

I quit the district after experiencing many restrictions in the classroom, but I have not quit being a teacher. It did not take long for me to conclude that the district is not interested in educating all students fairly, inclusively, and equitably. The district is also not interested in someone else teaching so-called marginalized students. As a student of thirteen years within the district, I was passed along grade levels for my age and not my knowledge. My "sentence with the district" began in first grade when I sat with other monolingual Spanish-speaking students and did nothing while the rest of the class learned English. The five or six of us sat around looking at each other in silence waiting for instruction. One day I realized that I needed to hustle my way to the English side of the class. While we sat around in silence and the rest of the class prepared for a spelling test, I took out my pencil and a blank sheet of paper. As the teacher began to dictate the words, I began to copy from the student closest to me. Because we were invisible to the teacher, she did not realize that I was copying. I purposely misspelled words to avoid being accused of copying. At the end of the test, I raised my hand and submitted my work. The adult teacher's aide took my paper and was extremely surprised that I was able to spell certain words. The other students at the table looked at me in amazement. The aide took the test to the teacher and suggested that I be moved to the English side of the room. Without much thought, the teacher agreed. I walked over with a smirk on my face and turned to my fellow classmates, suggesting that they too needed to copy in order to be promoted to the English side of the class. That was my first memory of hustling. I was the proud age of six.

As I ventured through the system, I realized that too many of my teachers were there only waiting to retire. In too few of my classes, I was able to experience a fluid exchange of ideas and information. It is ironic that my experience as a student was no different from that as a teacher. Administration constantly placed restrictions on what I was able to teach. I was observed so often by administration that I learned to distinguish the sound of students walking in the hallway to that of administration. The minute I heard administration walking the hallway, I knew they were coming to my class. My experience became so oppressive that I would often imagine being removed physically from the class right before my students. I became paranoid and felt imprisoned within my own class. The last two years I struggled to maintain my sanity, fighting not to be a *lifer*; teachers who have stayed in education for the salary and benefits at the cost of losing themselves. These teachers have given up on the profession. Their sole incentive for teaching is their retirement package. I refused to see myself as a *lifer*. A few of these *lifers* would remind me on a regular basis that my energy and idealism reminded them of themselves when they first started teaching. It would scare me to think that I could end up like them, cynical and sarcastic. I began to notice signs where I was turning into a *lifer*. When I first began teaching, I would assign essay finals. Every one of my mentors discouraged me from giving essay finals, "It takes too long to grade," or "scantrons make life so much easier." At the time, it did not make sense that I give a multiple-choice test for a social science exam. At the second school where I taught, they went as far as creating standardized tests. It was ridiculous but I followed it in order to avoid additional confrontation. We needed to teach to the test in order to improve the scores. I struggled to not get caught in that trap. I could not teach to a standardized test. Like a prison, everything was becoming standardized and the warden was always right. It became about having control of the students as well as teachers, and creativity was evaporating into thin air. Creativity was becoming something of the past. Limitations on free thinking were justified with the notion that, "this is a public school and the curriculum is set." Everyday I took a major risk by focusing on free thinking. If students could not think for themselves, they would be manipulated everyway possible for the rest of their lives.

Like prison, students are not permitted to question authority. The current trend of requiring school uniforms adds to the institutionalizing of a child's physical being and mind. Granted, students are giving fashion too much importance during school hours, but that is not the point for the uniform requirement. The uniform policy in public schools is being mandated in order to decrease gang affiliation. In recent years, I have witnessed random dogs sniffing backpacks and the use of handheld metal detectors inside classrooms. Random classes are selected and every third student is requested to step outside. They are searched from head to toe. Faculty and staff are expected to comply with this new prison like system of searching for drugs. Too often I found myself placing focus on enforcing the rules that were created by administration, which were seldom enforced by them. I was just like a prison guard. I am not suggesting that the existing drug problem in schools be ignored – that is another issue altogether. My concern is the oppressive environment that is being created. This is not the way to handle issues and create an environment conducive to learning and teaching.

On July 6, 2007 I ended my sentence with the district and walked away before becoming a *lifer*. In freeing myself I regained my freedom to speak and think without being written up. My decision to leave an environment that is bleak and oppressive might seem easy, but the reality is otherwise. My calling for teaching is one that will not permit me to sell out on the students or my ideologies. I decided that I would walk away from the district but not from education.

About the Author

Alberto "Beto" Gutierrez is a former high school social science teacher in the Los Angeles Unified School District. He teaches at a community college in the San Fernando Valley and at California State University, Northridge.

Beto is a student of cultures, which has led him to become a world traveler. He has visited over 20 countries within three continents. Through his travels, Beto has discovered their rich history often omitted from textbooks published within the United States' educational material.

Since the initial publication of this book, Beto has engaged in a second project where he highlights key travel experiences. In addition, Beto is working on a documentary focusing on the effects of gang violence.

To contact Beto for public speaking events or for his participation in educational forums, please send an email to beto911@yahoo.com or visit www.myspace/beto911.

www.ingramcontent.com/pod-product-compliance
Lightning Source LLC
LaVergne TN
LVHW092317080426
835509LV00034B/590